D1175844

RUTH PITTER:
HOMAGE TO A POET

RUTH PITTER:
HOMAGE TO A POET

Edited by Arthur Russell
With an introduction
by
David Cecil

Dufour Editions Inc.

LIBRARY OF CONGRESS
CATALOG NUMBER 77-88602

© 1969 ARTHUR RUSSELL
FIRST PUBLISHED 1969
IN THE UNITED STATES
OF AMERICA BY DUFOUR EDITIONS INC
CHESTER SPRINGS, PENNSYLVANIA
ORIGINALLY PUBLISHED IN GREAT BRITAIN
BY RAPP AND WHITING LTD
PRINTED IN ENGLAND BY
CLARKE, DOBLE AND BRENDON LTD
PLYMOUTH DEVON

CONTENTS

CONTENTS

ACKNOWLEDGMENTS

Acknowledgments are due to Ruth Pitter for published and unpublished material; to Cresset Press of London and Macmillans of New York for the many quotations from her collection *Poems 1926–1966*; to *Poetry Northwest* and the authors for the contribution by Stanley Kunitz and part of that by Carolyn Kizer; to the *Massachusetts Review* for Robin Skelton's; and to the authors for all the other contributions, which were written especially for this book. John Wain's essay was composed for us, after he had interviewed Ruth Pitter for radio; but, by agreement, it was first published in *The Listener*.

Some of the material in the biographical sketch 'Faithful to Delight' is from the texts of scripted and unscripted broadcasts for the BBC.

The title page device was specially designed by Joan Hassall. Norman Garner's portrait is from photographs and from life.

EDITOR'S FOREWORD

Twenty years or so is no exceptional time to have been a devotee of Ruth Pitter's, and I am a newcomer compared to some whose names are here. It is good to welcome others who are young enough to be our children or even grandchildren.

For me one of the best rewards from compiling this book has been that of finding myself among 'the blood-relations of the mind' as she has written. We have homed on her signal, and some of us now have more friends than when we started.

It has been a delight to see how eagerly many have responded. My warm thanks to all, and especially to Lord David Cecil whose instant applause at the start encouraged me to go ahead; and Mary Grieve whose staunch support later gave me a brave boost when it was needed.

Ruth Pitter's work is large enough to allow plenty of room both for agreement and disagreement. Some conflicting views will be found side by side here. But considering that I made hardly any attempt to suggest beforehand who should do what, there has been surprisingly little overlap. Where it does occur, it seems to me to add interest. Twice the same stanza has been selected by two different contributors; since each has different things to say about it, I have printed the stanza in full each time. In one or two other cases I have included a whole poem where the contributor had selected only a part. This I believe helps our book to achieve one of its purposes, since not all it readers will also have beside them a complete Pitter.

Books take many months to mature and appear, so in November 1968, for Ruth Pitter's seventy-first birthday, we told her about this one and gave her in token a greeting card made up from the signatures of all the contributors at that date. Now the book is complete and we can say :

Dear Ruth Pitter, please accept this act of homage.

TWO BLESSINGS

I am delighted to hear that you and others are paying tributes to Ruth Pitter's poetry, and am as always one of those who count her among the true poets of the period. A personality so fine duly finds such expression. I am getting old and can only, with apologies, send you these few words. But with many I shall rejoice in the honours paid to Ruth Pitter.

Edmund Blunden

I warmly approve of what you are undertaking. Ruth Pitter well deserves the tribute.

Andrew Young

INTRODUCTION

David Cecil

It is a pleasure and a privilege to introduce a collection of tributes to the art of Ruth Pitter. For me, she is the most moving of living English poets, and one of the most original. Not in the obvious sense of the word: there is nothing *avant-garde* or experimental about her work. On the contrary some of it, like Blake's *Poetical Sketches*, is deliberately written in the idiom of an older tradition. But – again like the *Poetical Sketches* – it never gives the impression of mere pastiche. Intensely alive, Miss Pitter always speaks with the voice of one living today and with immediate intimacy.

Surprisingly enough, this impression of vitality comes largely from her 'traditional' style. It allows her to make use of its full range of the language from the formal archaic to the modern colloquial. She seems not to bother whether a phrase is old-fashioned or new-made, but is only concerned that it should exactly convey her meaning. In a poem like 'The Military Harpist' she moves from ancient to modern with bold accomplishment.

> Strangely assorted, the shape of song and the bloody man.

> Under the harp's gilt shoulder and rainlike strings,
> Prawn-eyed, with prawnlike bristle, well-waxed moustache,
> With long tight cavalry legs, and the spurred boot
> Ready upon the swell, the Old Sweat waits.

Now dies, and dies hard, the stupid, well-relished
  fortissimo,
Wood-wind alone inviting the liquid tone,
The voice of the holy and uncontending, the harp.

Ceasing to ruminate interracial fornications,
He raises his hands, and his wicked old mug is David's,
Pastoral, rapt, the king and the poet in innocence,
Singing Saul in himself asleep, and the ancient Devil
Clean out of countenance, as with an army of angels.

The individual flavour of Miss Pitter's style comes mainly
from the way it combines vividness with precision, fusing
the two in a phrase at once unexpected and fastidiously apt:
as when she speaks of 'the delicate fox on soft and savage
feet' or 'the long blessed eventless days' of summer or 'the
elegiac spray' of the jasmine plant. Always the vividness of
her sensual apprehension is disciplined and clarified by intellectual precision.

The quality of her vision is as individual as is her use of
language. Two strains characterise it. The first is her response
to the natural world. This like everything else about her is
precise; she has an accurate, almost a scientist's knowledge
of the country scene: she looks with the eye of a naturalist
at flowers, animals, birds. Here she is describing a Stormcock.

Scarcely an arm's-length from the eye,
  Myself unseen, I saw him there;
The throbbing throat that made the cry,
  The breast dewed from the misty air,
The polished bill that opened wide
And showed the pointed tongue inside:

The large eye, ringed with many a ray
  Of minion feathers, finely laid,
The feet that grasped the elder-spray:
  How strongly used, how subtly made

The scale, the sinew, and the claw,
Plain through the broken roof I saw;

The flight-feathers in tail and wing,
The shorter coverts, and the white
Merged into russet, marrying
The bright breast to the pinions bright,
Gold sequins, spots of chestnut, shower
Of silver, like a brindled flower.

The second characteristic strain in Miss Pitter's poems is a religious strain, an intense awareness of a spiritual universe lying beyond the visible appearance of things. Sometimes this inspires her to a flight of symbolic imagination as in 'The Unicorn' or 'Six Dreams and a Vision'. More typically it blends with her response to the natural world: like some other English artists, like Vaughan and Samuel Palmer, Ruth Pitter is a Christian mystic of nature, seeing natural beauty as an image, an incarnation of a Divine reality.

And the tall flower was peace made visible,
The air was ambient love; the flashing fly
Was the soul's dear mysterious parable,
Proclaiming the immortal silently.

Two things in these lines are especially characteristic of their author. First she describes the air as 'ambient love': for her as for other Christian mystics, Divine reality means Divine love. Equally typical is her emphasis on peace and silence. Miss Pitter is not the poet of action or the crowded world. On the contrary, the world of her beatific vision is a place of contemplation, of solitude and silence, of moonlight and twilight, of rest and fruition – all harmonised in a mood of rapt still intensity. But her moments of full vision are rare. More often she has to be content with a hope or a memory of them that make her acutely aware of the discrepancy between the soul's desire and the bleak and hampering facts of human existence.

This awareness finds voice in her poetry; she sighs wistfully
for those moments when the tree and the bird reveal themselves, not just as tree and bird, but as the manifestation of
the spiritual force which gives them their being.

> They shine, they sing to the soul,
>   And the soul replies;
> But the inner love is not whole,
>   And the moment dies.
>
> O give me before I die
>   The grace to see
> With eternal, ultimate eye,
>   The Bird and the Tree.

At other times Miss Pitter's sense of a discord in the nature
of things is harsher and more positive. She is far too strong
a spirit not to face the fact that human experience is
evil and ugly. A poem like 'Funeral Wreaths' states with grim
irony her sense that man's longing for ideal beauty is all too
often distorted and vulgarised by the circumstances in which
he has been forced to live.

> In the black bitter drizzle, in rain and dirt,
> The wreaths are stacked in the factory entrance-yard.
> People gather about them. Nobody's hurt
> At the rank allusion to death. Down on the hard
> Cobblestones go the painted girls on their knees
> To read what the football-club has put on the card.
> There is interest, and delight, and a sense of ease.
> Is it only that flowers smell sweet, and are pretty and
>   bright,
> Or because of the senseless waste of so many pounds,
> Or because in that dreadful place the unwonted sight
> Of a heap of blossom is balm to unconscious wounds –
> The mortal wounds that benumb, not the sharp raw
>   pains
> Of the daily misery, but the fatal bleeding inside?

This poem was written in war-time. Living through two wars and an interval of peace hardly less dreadful, she has been profoundly affected by them. For her they are a dreadful testimony to the fact that man lives in a world which, though Divinely created, is now a fallen place where the forces of evil often triumph over the forces of love. So often that there are moments when she is tempted to despair. In her poem entitled '1938' she cries:

> If only the grave can calm us:
> If there my bones and my brother's
> Lying in peace, united,
> Bring no reproach on the mother
> Nor stir the father to anger:
>
> Let us go down together,
> Having despaired of wisdom:
> The earth is as fruitful as ever,
> The sea still teeming with fishes,
> The sun still lusty; but we
> Have failed to love, and must perish.

At such times she dreams of the peace that death might bring to the anguished spirit. But never for long! Her faith is too firmly rooted in the depths of her experience to be swept away by the flooding tide of despair. In her most sustained poem 'The Cygnet', two swans sailing down the Thames the morning after an air raid in London stand as a symbol for the victory of the soul over evil circumstance.

> It is broad day; on the polluted river,
> Thick with impurity yet crowned with honour,
> There sails a creature raised above pollution,
> Proud and immaculate as winter ermine,
> He who was last year's Cygnet; now from greyness
> Wholly redeemed; like the stream's peerless lily
> He opens to the struggling sun his pinions,
> Evoking from below the answering image.

Anger is past with him; the hissing madness
Of unrequited passion is forgotten:
See where she glides, and turns that look upon him
Which only death extinguishes once kindled;
For they like every noble thing are faithful,
Finding in love the only cure of sorrow,
Abandoning themselves each to the other,
Losing the separate self, the seed of anguish.

Go, vanish into the far secret places,
With the bright signature of love upon you;
Gathering in your breasts the sacred river
Of life, which through your royal blood flows onward,
Blooming in snow and fire, fulfilled for ever:
While we, still bound in anger and pollution,
Battle through dreary days and nights of terror
Until our spirit flowers, and we follow.

Certainly Miss Pitter's own spirit has flowered; and all the
more beautifully for 'the dreary days and nights of terror'
that it has endured. Strong and tender, it has been illuminated
by the suffering they brought; and made her words at once
more poignant and more consoling. It is because we recognise
that she herself has faced the full brunt of our tormented age
that we listen to her when she calls to us.

Die unaccursed though the universal
curse be abroad: for of her God remembered
though the world burn, the spirit as a bird shall
flee to her mountain.

FAITHFUL TO DELIGHT : A PORTRAIT SKETCH

Arthur Russell

The proudest day of Ruth Pitter's life was when at the age of fifty-seven she received the Queen's Gold Medal for Poetry from the hands of Her Majesty at Buckingham Palace.

She had bought a new pink hat and had brushed her best dark suit, a very good one, passed on by a wealthy friend; and the village taximan had driven her nearly fifty miles to the Palace. There the Queen presented the Medal and talked with her for ten minutes, mostly about her writing and her daily life.

Later, at a private luncheon in town with a few friends, the great gold piece lay gleaming in the centre of the table; it is over two inches across, and bears on one side the Queen's head, and on the other a delicate nude figure by Edmund Dulac. After a good meal and wine there was a cake iced by one of the guests and garnished with a spray of poetaz, the narcissus that grows on Mount Parnassus. 'But when we got home,' she says, 'didn't we rush to put the kettle on!'

A few weeks before that, John Masefield, then Poet Laureate, had telephoned to tell her of the award (which had been left in abeyance during the War). It was because Ruth Pitter was the first woman to receive it that Her Majesty broke precedent and presented it in person. One of the Laureate's duties was to make recommendations for the award to his Sovereign, as he liked to call her. He acted on the advice of a committee; that year it consisted of Nevill Coghill, Walter de la Mare, Charles Morgan, Gilbert Murray, Vita Sackville-West, Sir Osbert Sitwell, and himself. He was able to tell Miss Pitter that they had been unanimous.

She seldom recalls the day of the Medal without thinking 'How I wish my good mother and father could have been there!'

They were schoolteachers, and they never stopped teaching. 'They didn't just give us poetry, they taught it to us' she has written; and in particular the *Golden Treasury*, Blake's *Songs of Innocence*, Wordsworth's Lucy poems, and Shakespeare's songs. 'They made us notice special beauties, and they made us learn poems by heart; but they paid us for this extra work, from a penny to sixpence a poem according to length.' As she says, this is a wonderful way to stock the mind at its most retentive age, 'wax to receive, marble to retain'. She seldom needs a book on a train journey; and the poetry she knows by heart has a special consolatory quality – 'it's like being able to put on a record: in some dreadful situation, such as waiting in a hospital, you can switch it on and repeat it to yourself, and you are in a world apart.'

Both parents taught as assistants in elementary schools in the East End of London; they were good and sympathetic at the job and would have made good head teachers, she thinks. It was hard work, for standards were high, and the pupils so badly fed and housed that it was difficult to stir their minds.

Ruth was the eldest of the family. She was born on 7 November 1897 in the new eastern suburb of Ilford. Not long afterwards the family followed the outward spread of mono-tonous new suburbs to Goodmayes; and here, at the age of five, she was sent to the elementary school which had perhaps a thousand pupils. 'That huge crowd of children, some of them pretty savage, appalled me, but I was strong, and soon learnt to be belligerent because I was afraid.'

By this time she had a younger sister, Olive, and a brother, Geoffrey. Mrs Pitter found that she could not keep house for five on her husband's small pay, and she returned to teaching at about thirty-five shillings a week, while Geoffrey was still an infant. A young aunt who came to live with them was a great comfort, for she could cook well and was good at entertaining the children with tales and tricks.

As they grew old enough for walks, they were taken to Hainault Forest, part of the ancient hunting forest of Epping that begins where the suburbs end. It was a long trudge from Goodmayes, but sometimes they would go part of the way by train or station fly. Hainault became their favourite playground; the whole family would picnic there on fine Saturdays, and Ruth and her father would tramp the woods all day at any time of year. Later the family managed to rent an old decayed cottage on Crabtree Hill in the forest. They came to look on this as home, though it was primitive and comfortless compared with their small suburban house; and it appears again and again in Ruth's poems. This was the real centre of their life for many years; the town family became rural by adoption.

It was 'a joyful infancy'. The earliest things she can clearly recollect are her first bird's nest, her first red toadstool, and a bare green hill at sunset. Here began the natural mysticism that has been the light of her work and life.

Brought up with poetry, all three children tried to write it, but only Ruth went on. Olive is now the successful novelist Shirley Murrell, and Geoffrey, a retired architect and surveyor, is a sparetime painter of distinction, who has affinities with Lowry and Dufy.

21

Ruth herself was five when she wrote her first poem. 'I was sitting on the back doorstep' she relates 'when suddenly there came into my mind, overwhelmingly, an image of something we had seen on one of our walks – a desolate and abandoned place. It was the first thing that ever gave me a poetic sensation. My eyes filled with tears of a strange new kind. Seizing my stump of blue pencil and a bit of torn paper I began in painful capitals: "The old mill stands with broken shaft . . ." I think that line is fairly poetical, but not the rest of it.' She still has some of these early verses in blue pencil and block letters.

She has defined a poet as 'a person who has *seen something* and has got to tell someone about it . . . This astonishing gift of special seeing is quite common among children. To this extent perhaps most children are poets. As we grow up it is generally lost. I can remember so well, from earliest childhood, seeing something in the light on a hill, or in the shape of a flower, or in a human face (perhaps a very plain face) which seemed absolutely heavenly. It was so strong a feeling that I felt I must tell the world about it or burst. Ordinary description was no use; poetry it had to be.'

She was teased both at home and at school about her poetry making, but in time (she says) this taught her a measure of cunning and ruthlessness. In her teens, her writing both advanced her and held her back.

Her secondary school was much nearer the city centre, but from the laboratory on the top floor she could see the wooded skyline of Hainault and Epping and yearn for them: 'I wanted to "fade away into the forest dim" and stay there all my life . . .'

It was in her twelfth year that she moved to the Coborn School at Bow, an old Christian charity school which had originally sent girls out to domestic service, and therefore still insisted on 'manners'. Her sister had earned the coveted allowance of £10 a year in the County Scholarship examination, which took her on to the County High School and thence to a degree at the London School of Economics. Ruth had failed to earn the allowance, so her mother sent her to the Coborn. This had some advantages, for she gained a good smattering of Latin and an abiding love of Horace; the art class too was ahead of its time, and the cookery class very good.

She suffered from the daily journey to the real East End, and the school's stinking factory surroundings; and also from scrappy feeding – 'part poverty, part ignorance'. The pupils were much more varied than at her earlier school. She did not do particularly well – the pressures within her were always greater than those from outside – but she managed to matriculate.

One handicap may well have been her early success in getting published. Her father was pleased and proud to watch the precocious child absorbed in her writing: 'One day he took me as a cat takes a kitten in his mouth, and showed me to an editor, Orage, who printed some of my work. I was then not quite fourteen years old.'

A. R. Orage, then about thirty-seven, edited New Age, a socialist weekly of considerable influence though small circulation. Katharine Mansfield was another of the many young writers that he discovered. For the next twenty years or so Ruth Pitter's poems were constantly appearing in his pages, and in the New English Weekly which succeeded the New Age.

Did the two men act unwisely? Certainly they encouraged a large output of immature verse, much of it highly skilled and almost wholly imitative. Praise and encouragement were valuable at that formative age, in a life not much privileged. But one feels that nothing – not even a total lack of response from anyone – could have stemmed this flow of essential practice work. Premature publication merely stimulated. A more varied stock of models to imitate might have helped an earlier maturity. As it was her father, who held the *Golden Treasury* sacred, insisted at first on making schoolmasterly corrections to her work, in spite of her strong disapproval.

'It is perhaps characteristic of youth', she has written, 'that I used more elaborate and complicated rhythms than in maturity. It does not take much to make a child into a mere specialist, concentrating on technical performance; it is a kind of strength much more quickly acquired than real ripeness.'

Orage was an authority on Nietzsche, and in later years a prophet of Social Credit. He was unable to pay his contributors, but he passed on ideas – Freud's for instance. Ruth Pitter once related: 'My good old editor Orage was always in search of anything new. He ran through the cults hungrily, and when he came up against Freud's theories it wasn't long before I heard of them. When I was eighteen or so, he gave me a great fat book, I think it was Ernest Jones's first book, to read; and I at once joined in the delightful game of catching other people out and catching oneself out. I think this is a bad thing in a way; it stultifies one: you anticipate your own errors, and so never commit them, and tend to get nowhere. You lose the experience of your failures.' A recent comment is more sombre: 'The real thing was the traumatic experience – those case-histories! It took years to get over. But I then knew a lot more about how we are motivated, and this was very salutary'.

When World War One broke out she was nearly seventeen and in the Intermediate Arts class, which might have led on to university; but there was no question of going on, for in those days such a family could not afford it unless the child was 'clever' enough to win scholarships. Wilfred Owen was in the same case, and many another. Sometimes she still regrets the lack of a university education but she has come to accept that she may have been better without it, as she is no student.

'I was brought up to worry about money', she says. 'I was born into a world where you could easily starve through no fault of your own.' Livelihood was precarious. Her parents would ask her: 'If you don't marry and you're not going to be a teacher how on earth are you going to live?' This sank in and remained. 'And there was so large a surplus of young women', she points out, 'that we knew very well we couldn't all marry – and we liked the idea of independence.'

With no career in view, it seemed natural in 1914 to seek war work. She got herself a junior temporary clerkship in the War Office at twenty-five shillings a week. The staff were kind and good to her, but she hated the paperwork and was unhappy until she took over the tea-making for about fifty people. This took a lot of time and gave her satisfaction. The job lasted a couple of years, but by then she was in poor health and left. What to try next?

Having vague thoughts of trying to become some kind of artist, she found employment after a time with a couple called Jennings, artist and architect, who lived on the Suffolk coast and managed even in wartime to make simple furniture and other wares, and decorate them in pleasant styles still seen on the Continent.

She lived with them and was taught these crafts. At first she received only her keep, but later a little pay; she was content to be learning how to use wood-working tools, and the ABC of painting. It is significant that one grandfather was a master cabinetmaker, and the other a toolmaker, which may help to explain the boldly practical side of her nature and her many hand-skills. 'Working with the hands', she has said, 'has always seemed to me the only satisfactory way of earning a living. It soothes the mind, while brainwork teases it to shreds.' It also allows her to compose.

The war ended, her employers moved to London, and she moved with them. At first she lived with them again; but at twenty-two she resolved to have a place of her own. With £50 earned in her spare time, she took two rooms over their workshop in a mews, bought some odds and ends of furniture, and became a householder.

By 1930 the slump had made her employment intermittent and precarious. A similar business, or what remained of it, was offered to her. Alone she would not have ventured, but a friend and fellow-worker, the artist Kathleen O'Hara, ten years her senior, egged her on. Pooling their savings – between £500 and £600 – they had just enough to start. At first they kept their two little flats, but later took over the whole house where the business was, and lived over the workshop. Once having set up housekeeping together, they have been together ever since.

They had much to learn: 'We knew how to produce the goods but not how to buy, sell, keep accounts, or get business; and we soon found there was nothing to be done but get a travelling salesman and supply the trade.' They got a good traveller at the second attempt, and after six months they began to do well.

One early disaster led to a fortunate result. During very hot weather Ruth was opening a can of old acetate paint left by the previous owners, when the lid blew off into one eye. She needed hospital treatment and had both eyes blindfolded for two months. During this time she had a sudden vision of something she had quite forgotten: a close-up of a misselthrush in full song in February, studied through the broken roof of the Hainault cottage years before . . . 'Stormcock in Elder', recollected bindfold and written down later, has appeared in more anthologies than any other poem of hers. 'It wasn't worth it', she now says – 'horrible accident and at such an anxious time.'

The demand for painted furniture had dropped away. Trays and numerous other 'gift goods', painted with flowers, now sold best, and for Ruth painting ousted woodwork. At first both partners painted, but as the trade grew, 'K' O'Hara found herself fully engaged in buying, seeing customers, and giving out work and orders. Ruth stuck to the bench and the book-keeping. They still boast that theirs were the best painted gift goods in the trade.

By the outbreak of war in 1939 they had a thriving busi-ness and employed twelve or more people. The good traveller and several skilled girls left immediately for war work, and others were called up one by one. Imported wares were used up; then the night blitz reduced working hours, and twice the glass roof of the workshop was blown in. The remaining staff worked at home.

At the fall of France when the British were left alone, Ruth went to the Labour Exchange and offered to do anything; but the war machine was not then fully in action, there was still a lot of unemployment, and she was not wanted. However, a time came when Ruth's age-group was due to register. Directed labour meant liability to be sent anywhere, perhaps losing one's home; so the two friends crossed the river from the artists' quarter of Chelsea to the industrial south side, and found themselves work that was part of the 'war effort'.

'Indeed we have no choice but to go over', she wrote at the time; but though Ruth had to satisfy the authorities, she has never forgotten that K, being then over fifty and so not liable for directed labour, need not have gone over with her.

They worked in a dark factory that (among other things) made crucibles – 'simple as doom, made to endure the furnace'. Both had office jobs, but Ruth took one evening shift a week in a machine shop 'to show willing'; she was turning carbon rods on a lathe. 'I learnt a lot in that shop', she says, 'and shed some bitter tears there; but I wouldn't have missed it. The factory was very dirty and I got rheumatism and dermatitis. "Lousy dump but lovely people" was the general verdict, which I endorse. It was a wonder to me to see the beauty, and indeed the moral beauty, of many of that old industrial population.' Here she saw, but never spoke to, the beautiful young red-headed Irishwoman whose death from bombing is mourned in two stanzas of 'The Cygnet' – 'the high Milesian wonder, in whom the life like summer lightning played, and whose passion leaped abroad in flashes . . .'

K, worn out with overwork and fire-fighting, left the factory when war ended. Ruth stayed on for several months. In spite of her hatred of paperwork she had taken on the job of looking after the insurance cards of all the 5,000 employees of the factory. She had found them in great confusion, as this was the time of the fly-bombs and rockets on London. Employees surged back and forth, leaving the job and returning, and some acquired three or four insurance cards. Things were fairly straight when she left.

Wartime winters were grim enough for London factory workers. Ruth reached her own nadir after a day on which a man had fallen down the factory lift-shaft: 'I stopped in the middle of Battersea Bridge one dreadful March night, when it was cold and the wind was howling over the bridge, and it was dark as the pit; and I leaned over the parapet and thought: Like this I cannot go on. I must find somebody or something. Like this I cannot go on.'

The answer came some months afterwards, when she heard the lively religious broadcasts of C. S. Lewis and as she says 'grappled them to her soul'. She assembled family and friends to hear him, for simple enjoyment, and she read every word of his that she could find. By hard argument she convinced herself that his Christian message was what she needed: 'I had to be intellectually satisfied as well as emotionally, because at that time of one's life one doesn't just fall into religion with adolescent emotion. But at last I was satisfied at every point that it was the one way for me. It wasn't the easy road but it was the only possible one.' That was said some years ago; now she is humbler: 'I haven't any arguments; it only seems that love will have it so.'

She had some Roman Catholic friends who saw her crisis and tried quite fairly to persuade her into their way of thinking. She attended a series of lectures by a lady who propounded Cardinal Newman's doctrine of Assent. Newman demands action following belief, and this animated in Ruth the ideas which had been accepted from Lewis but not acted upon. (One of her most splendidly musical poems, 'On a Certain Philosophy', reflects the debate within herself: 'Out of the order, the calm, the mighty conclusions/Breathe as of balm, sing triumph, like adamant shine . . .')

Her mother too had been through a phase of leaning towards Rome – but this was only one of what the family then called the 'fancy religions' that she dabbled in. As for her father, she has described him as a 'mild Fabian agnostic'. But though neither was an active churchgoer, both had been brought up as Christians and trained at Anglican colleges, and they had had all three children baptised in one batch into the Church of England, perhaps because this was the only way in which they could qualify for certain scholarships.

At the crossroads of her spiritual life, Ruth clung to that baptism: 'As I had to make up my mind, I thought: I will belong to the traditional church of my country. Never mind about Henry VIII; it is the church into which I was born and into which I was baptised, in however lighthearted a manner. That is the church for me.' So in her forties she decided to be confirmed; but even when recalling so solemn a decision the comic will break in: 'And so I went to the old parson where we then had our country home, and said I wished to be confirmed. He was so pleased that he at once produced a very rich confirmation veil from a bottom drawer and flung it over his delicious prey with a gesture of delight . . .'

There was nothing frivolous about her conversion and she found it a long process – 'it's a dreadful thing to get religion in middle age because there's so much to be undone; so much to be pulled down before it can be built up again.' What in particular had to be undone, she found, was the egoism of all artists.

In another vein she has written: 'A late-come Christian like me is always to some extent set in a bad shape, and must hobble in the rear, getting along as it can on its self-distorted legs. It is very disappointed when it comes to heel after such years of self-pleasing, thinking that in return for its submission it will be kindly received, fostered, taken care of: only to find the church almost as disappointing as the world outside, and depending on one's own contribution.'

Perhaps she has described this contribution of her own in describing some of its rewards: 'Love of the neighbour without idolatry; enormous sweetness and delight in the fellow-creature, and in being sometimes able to return good for evil — to be serene in the face of what makes poor humanity so often blow up.'

That is part of her daily life. Outside it, her poems both secular and religious can solace even hardy non-believers; and this too, surely, is a Christian act.

Ruth had been frightened and worried about starting the business, but K's courage carried them forward at that time. Once they were making good money Ruth's anxiety faded: 'I found I could write a little poetry every day, with tears of gratitude and enjoyment.' K's instinct served them well. Beginning in the slump, with their slender resources, they made enough in the ten years up to 1940 to buy a house later on. After the war they did not resume trading in the old way. Some of their former staff had started on their own, and the new taxes and restrictions were difficult. Ruth still retained a few old customers, and she decided to work at home, since she could sell all that she did. This she has continued right up to the present time, but the business has gradually tapered off. Customers have died or given up their shops, and it has become more difficult to get both the goods and the right materials. 'And of course', she points out sensibly, 'there's the modern idea that things should not be ornamented so much – they should contain their own beauty without addition. This is fair enough. My work's served me well for almost half a century so I don't grudge its coming to an end.'

She uses quick-drying cellulose paints, and fibreglass trays have supplanted the more sympathetic papiermaché, no longer obtainable. Her modern paint and modern mercury-vapour lamp both provided brilliant ideas for late poems. Her painting seat is now a typist's swivelling steel chair of the latest design, adjustable for height and posture. She works facing a window with a view of garden and birds; there is no table in front of her, but a couple of stools carry brushes and materials. Holding each tray in her lap she paints freehand and rapidly. After so long at it she can design as she goes, laying on one colour at a time wherever it is needed over the whole pattern, then setting it aside to dry. Four or more nearly flat shades of green may go to the modelling of a single leaf.

Her work bears comparison with the best flower-painting on porcelain. Though stylised, it has a poet-botanist's realism that Andrew Young must approve. On one small tray she may show the wild strawberry fruit at three distinct stages of ripeness, as well as bud and flower. Yet she achieves her effects by a shorthand of crisp strokes and blobs, each meaningful and none niggling. The result is always graceful and delicate; only on examining it closely does one realise that it is achieved by bold and even dashing brushwork. No design that she paints in her seventies has the air of tired repetition; each petal, leaf and stem looks as if the painter had made a fresh close scrutiny of the original.

The same intent eye is at work in both her arts. Young Paris, in one poem, has a 'voracious eye'; it might be her own, for she writes elsewhere of 'my all-devouring eyes'. There are other glimpses of her: 'perusing death with these shade-coloured eyes'; 'the summer eyes that can both weep and burn'. In a poem from a low point of her middle life, a shadowy catechist asks her: 'Did you see the fine sights, with your good clear eyes?' and the reply reveals a fear that this splendid eyesight may waste away with her muscles. But half a lifetime later we find her gazing into a flower, 'putting an eye too close until it blurs'; and on the next page we are startled to see her '. . . stare in an eye, hold the soul still to read it by'.

Only when 'the insupportable eye of the furnace glares' is she outfaced.

For a time after the war the partners remained Londoners. K is urban, but Ruth always hated the noise and dirt, and the anxieties of business. She now had another country base. This was a cottage at Felstead in Essex which her mother had bought on retirement in 1930, four years after her husband's death. Mrs Pitter died in 1941, and Ruth's widowed sister lived on at Felstead for eleven more years, before a second marriage took her away and the cottage had to be sold. It had one peculiarity, an enormous vinery. Here Ruth taught herself how to grow and train and prune the vine: 'it's a matter of great precision – every bud matters. I think I could go back and do it in the dark, simply by feeling the buds . . .' The judgment between one growth and another, the shape of the vine's leaf and scent of its flower, the rewarding harvest – these gave her a deep satisfaction and she regretted leaving them behind. 'The years have no weight when the holy vine is in bloom.'

In 1952 the partners packed up and bought a house in the country, in the large straggling village of Long Crendon, within reach of their friends in Oxford and others. Long Crendon has been transformed into an upper-middle class preserve, with most of the charming old stone and timbered cottages 'restored' and turned into model residences. Ruth and

K did not follow this fashion, but bought a plain solid brick house, then about forty years old, set in 2½ acres of old nursery-garden and orchard.

Here Ruth's life expanded, but only by firmly combating incessant demands on her time: for the village is a social one – she has compared it to Cranford – and the old custom of 'calling' persisted. The land fulfilled a deep need. No longer dependent on hurried weekends in the country, she could watch and work in her huge garden every day of the year. The plant and bird life at her door has been 'an inexhaustible mine of felicity' after the long town years. ('But no vines! no forest!' she still grieves.)

She has called herself a compulsive gardener, and frankly begrudges the time spent on anything else. Organising what help she can from the village, often children or women who come for no more than an hour or two a week, she has created a casual and graceful domain with nothing formalised about it except the kitchen garden. There is much mown grass with daisies in it, and always plenty more in need of light or heavy mowing; carefully-tended flowers and others left to scramble for themselves; many old trees including a group of big crack-willow framing the orchard from the house; good shrubs left by the previous nurserymen; a sunny goldfish-pool with seats beside it for tea and talk, close to the overgrown and prolific apple-orchard. Flycatchers nest in the honeysuckle rioting over the large toolshed, and generations of swallows in its rafters.

But the kitchen garden is never casual. It is ruled with cunning and benevolent tyranny, and its ranks radiate the bursting energy of a marchpast of athletes. For years the two friends have eaten their own fruit and vegetables at all times, and visitors often depart laden.

Ruth's many manual skills include the use of the ancient scythe; the big English one with its crooked snaith she now finds rather too much for her, and she has taken gladly to the lightweight 'Turkish' type with a straight handle. She also has a love-hate relationship with her three motor-mowers, in spite of the fact that a moment's inattention with one of them cost her the top joint of a finger of her left hand.

For the poet, the move from London did not mark a productive period. However, the award of the Gold Medal in 1955 was followed by a number of broadcasts and a series of appearances in television Brains Trusts. She took to the cameras without fuss, contributed wisdom, fun, and repose, and gained a faithful following. ('That marvellous woman who used to be on TV?' asked an elderly bookbinder, seven years after her last appearance.) But she was too seldom allowed to develop the wide-ranging vivacity of her private conversation. This new, public Ruth Pitter later had a year of writing about gardening and religion for a mass-circulation women's magazine (see Mary Grieve, p. 58). Since these demands came to an end she has appeared little before the larger public, except in occasional sound broadcasts.

Such activities were marginal; they gave her money to spend and even to save, but did not encourage her to write poetry. In fact, a few years after the move to Crendon, she confessed that she had produced since then 'only a few wizened imps'. She told friends that she was a fulfilled artist and her task was complete. It was left to America to question her silence.

The poet Carolyn Kizer, editor of *Poetry Northwest*, published in Seattle, decided in 1960 to devote one issue to saluting Pitter. She wrote to ask whether the poet had any unpublished work. The result was dazzling. *Poetry Northwest**

* This issue of *Poetry Northwest* also included tributes from a number of fellow-poets. Carolyn Kizer's appears in part on p. 79 of the present volume, and that of Stanley Kunitz on p. 81; Thom Gunn has written a new essay which appears on p. 63. The tribute of the late John Holmes included this: 'Only the walking dead could not feel her fire at the touch. She is a master-craftsman, sustaining a voice of classical tradition, yet speaking in and of her times.'

was able to print for the first time seven poems, most of them showing her mastery at its highest. These became the nucleus of the 1966 volume *Still by Choice*.

This could hardly be called a turning-point in her career, like some that can be traced in earlier years. The first was Orage's encouragement. Some years later came Belloc's: not only did he write a preface for her (as did James Stephens and Masefield) but he published two of her earliest volumes at his own expense – a rare thing for even a rich poet to do for a novice. These early works have not been reprinted, for she decided long ago to keep nothing she had written much before the age of thirty. Another turning-point was the award of the Hawthornden Prize in 1937 for her first mature serious volume, *A Trophy Of Arms*. 'That brought me out into the daylight', she has said.

Such events and persons may have helped or harmed her output, but they had little influence on her style. There, one may note one or two other landmarks. First of these perhaps was her inevitable realisation that natural speech rhythms can be the basis of poetry, as in Old English alliterative and the sprung rhythm that Hopkins derived from it. She delights in both.

Another was Sir George Rostrevor Hamilton's book *The Telltale Article*. Before reading this she had made a lavish and unreflecting use of *the*, like many poets from the twenties onwards. ('The desert in the garden the garden in the desert of drouth, spitting from the mouth the withered apple-seed' is an example from Eliot.) No poems that she wrote after reading *The Telltale Article* suffer from the same affliction. But the book also helped her to make up her mind about Eliot himself, after a twenty-five years struggle.

She has tried to be fair to him, but her fairness is frosty. For example: 'I pay him all honour as a truly gifted poet, as a serious student and critic of poetry, and a man who must be treated with respect as having made very great innovations in English verse – though not I think to its advantage' (1955). Or this (1968): 'I am perfectly aware of his stature as much superior to my own, but an English cat may look at an American king.' (But she insists that her critical opinions are of little importance except to herself.)

She knew Eliot slightly, as a friend of the *New Age* set, a kind good man and a fellow Christian: they sometimes attended the same early Communion services at Chelsea Old Church. A week after she had been awarded the Queen's Medal, she recognised him in a bus queue, and he was able to present his courtly congratulations in person. It was an encounter that gave her real pleasure.

Eliot and Pitter both wrote books of cat-verse, and many readers like both. But she does not warm to Old Possum's rollicking nonsense-cats; his book appears 'rather old-maidish' to her.

Ruth Pitter On Cats (1947) is funny but practical. She shows an acute sympathy with the basic needs of real cats – food, procreation, and human servants. Of 'The Neuter Cat's Apotheosis' in which she gives the whole leg of a huge turkey to a poor old cottage-cat who had never had a full stomach in his life, she has said: 'I feel this poem is palpitatingly my own.'

There are two other books of what she calls her grotesques or babouineries – *A Mad Lady's Garland* (1934), accomplished parody and pastiche; and *The Rude Potato* (1941) – comic gardening verse, ribald at times. She is liable to break into praise of the limerick as an art-form, and claims to have composed some that are unprintable.

This dichotomy has troubled her more idealistic admirers. When *The Rude Potato* was offered to her American publisher he is (unreliably) reported to have said: 'For fifteen years I've been building you up as a dedicated spirit, and now look what you've done !' But for her there is no contradiction : there is beatitude in the bird of paradise and a delight 'wild, bracing, and inconsequent' in a potato of shameless form – 'so nourishing, so lewd'. In childhood her brother and sister noted gleefully that she wore the same look of grave absorption whether she was writing serious or comic verse. Medieval churchmen tricked out their cathedrals with bizarre hobgoblins, and she has hers. 'Alehouse mirth', she has written, 'can exist along with the grace, beauty and holiness of life. It is in fact a part of these, and its separation from the rest was a calamity. The problem is to free earthy humour from dreary dirt and bring it back where it belongs, a part of the real spiritual wealth of man.'

However, for most of her life she kept her different kinds of poetry in different books. Then in *Still by Choice* a few lightweights appeared beside the serious work; and soon afterwards in *Poems 1926–1966* she gathered the best of both kinds for the first time between the same covers. 'My old extravagances are as much a part of me as my ancestral fears and my immortal longings', she wrote. It was a reconciliation.

No book of hers has lost money for her publisher, but poetry has not been profitable. Her best earnings were over a short period, from television and journalism. From poetry proper she has reckoned on making £50 to £70 a year, mostly from anthology fees; the figure rose to £175 the year that she won the Hawthornden. She keeps it for luxuries – 'it's very nice money, you can buy a bottle of wine or go to the theatre with money like that.' But it will not buy her dream of material bliss – 'a bed with an oyster satin eiderdown, and a bell that I can ping to summon a domestic who will fetch me another champagne cocktail.' Miss O'Hara insists that this remark is quite false to Miss Pitter's nature. Miss Pitter stoutly disagrees; but on reflection she admits that perhaps it is not really her.

She quotes Samuel Butler – 'no gold, no Holy Ghost' – but it was mostly manual work that brought the gold, until her

37

year or two as a public performer. There is no repining. She applies her blunt good sense: 'The faculty of poetry is a gift of heaven, not a virtue. It is unethical to complain of neglect and low monetary rewards for poetry. If we want money we must produce something people will buy. If they don't want poetry we can't expect them to buy it.'

It would be possible to argue that Ruth Pitter is a man's poet. Certainly she has retained the admiration and friendship of many men, especially writers. Lord David Cecil has been her good friend and chief stimulus for over thirty years. With Orage, Æ, Masefield, Belloc, James Stephens, C. S. Lewis, Sir George Hamilton, and Sir Ronald Storrs, she was on friendly terms and corresponded until their deaths.

George Orwell (like Lord David, several years her junior) came in a different category. She first met him briefly as a tall schoolboy with formidable blue eyes that were an exact pair – a rare thing, she noted. When he left the Burma Police after five years, he surprised her by writing to ask if she and K could find him a cheap lodging. They found a room near their Bayswater workshop. It was a bitter winter; they did their best to help him, but he was difficult to help. They tried to get him to wear an overcoat, and managed to lend him an oil-heater when his hands were too cold to write. When he moved they let him keep a suitcase full of shabby clothes at their place; he would change there before some sortie into the underworld.

Sometimes he would ask Ruth to go out with him, but he was desperately poor and ill and he suffered at having to let her pay their bus fares or supply a picnic lunch. She found him good company on country walks in Suffolk where his parents and K's lived; and he also stayed once with the Pitters at their tumbledown cottage in the forest. But between 1935 and his death from tuberculosis in 1950 she saw him only once, when she visited him and his first wife, Eileen, in their damp basement flat. She never knew him as the very success-ful author he became in his last years.

'Orwell's great virtue', she has written, 'was that he would not let things go by default, as we nearly all do. He threw all his forces into the battle for truth. Once he was convinced that we had no business in Burma, out he came – never mind the sacrifice of his career. Time-serving in any form he hated and rejected with all his force. It was a pure scientific honesty very rare in literature.'

The perpetual menace of poverty in youth made her in her own words 'too much afraid of life.' At times she has fancied herself as a recluse, though of course a recluse with a garden. 'To be a poet', she has said, 'demands solitude and silence above everything. The one thing one wishes about other people is that they would go away.' But she recognised early that it would be neurotic to indulge such feelings, and learned instead the delight in her fellows that has inspired some of her most moving poetry.

Although she may argue that 'every creative woman needs a wife', she also holds that a woman poet may be better off without a husband. 'I felt that instinctively from the first' she said. 'I would look at the boy next door and I would look at young men met in the course of one's work, and say to myself that they simply were not relevant. One might be very fond of them; but it would have been cruelty to animals to marry them (supposing them to be willing) because there was always this ruling passion, this major preoccupation, in which the poor dears had no share. Of course, once one had made a little money one could have married middle-aged men very easily. The moment a single woman has a little money she has to look out for herself. I was always very firm; I never had the slightest illusion about that sort of set-up.' She blew her top with one of them who invoked her as a kind of art nouveau princess.

Her figure is stocky; her step, nimble and purposeful, is that of a much younger woman: 'she breathes a time-defying air'. The dark grey eyes, often preoccupied, gaze from a face surprisingly pale and unlined considering the weathering it gets.

The interior of the house is white, and on the white walls are many pictures, including a Rothenstein portrait of Ruth as a young woman, a seascape by Æ and landscapes by Geoffrey Pitter, and several of K's large flower paintings, grave, decorative and dreamlike. The furniture is a blend of excellent antique and nondescript useful, with one or two quiet modern pieces. Most meals are eaten in a central hall or passage-room, little more than an alcove, but with a snug stove and a mass-produced oak gate-leg table, its top scrubbed pale. The workroom is also the chief sitting room of the two friends, and it has Ruth's desk and typewriter as well as her painting gear and tray-racks.

Ruth Pitter has summed herself up in the preface to *Poems 1926–1966*: 'One has pursued a ruling passion, ignored what seemed irrelevant, earned a living somehow, lurked observant in the thorny undergrowth; never attained any earthly consolations to speak of, except the ineffable communion with the earth itself and some of its creatures; sorry for everybody and trying to be kind, yet privately boiling with those disgraceful rancours which are the exhaust-fumes of ruling passions . . .'

'I have tried to be faithful to delight, to beatitude, being unable to see what else can be absolutely significant . . .'

THE COOL CLEAR VOICE

John Arlott

To a young man in the 1930s, struggling to take in the poetry of his own time, Ruth Pitter provided the pleasures of variety and surprise. Her sense of literary tradition and background and eighteenth-century forms, in one so sharply of her own time; her reverence and irreverence; her high degree of technical skill – and the ability to mock it; her gravity and her humour, made reading her poetry a series of constantly fresh experiences.

Later I was to appreciate her sympathy towards younger writers, the care with which she read their work, the helpful pertinence of her criticism, her essential kindness. Her conversation has always and easily bridged the gap between ages and sexes because she never talks unless she has something to say: hers is the true economy of speech, she talks of universals and not of trivia. Her companionable sense of fun goes with a perception of enduring values and a respect for all humans. She is sensitive but she is also capable. The bony-structure of her face is strong as well as fine, her look is steady, her hands are neatly capable enough for the fine brushwork of her craft of decoration, and sturdy enough to dig her garden thoroughly.

It was most easy to appreciate her qualities under the stress of war, which she approached with calm realism. She would do what she could to help, up to the limits of her powers; but she refused to allow it to disturb the processes of her mind or to drive her, defensively, away from the apparently minor, but personally important, aspects of her life. She shed the trappings and shut out the intrusions of war when she came back to that deliberately simple house in Old Church Street, Chelsea, where values were not vulnerable to bombs.

A still sharp recollection of her comes from a war-time evening in the Church Street house, blacked-out but still with its own, particular, slightly austere, warmth. Somewhere not far away there was a blumping of guns or bombs, or both: I half listened for the noise to come nearer and then suddenly, found myself listening to her voice, not its words but its *sound* – which, in my mind, I can hear now as I heard it then – cool, level, yet sensitively modulated, firm, clear, reassuring. Suddenly the voice darted away with an idea and called me back to the words. It was, she threw out, impossible to have a sense of humour and to be a great poet. But what of Shakespeare? He was, as always, the exception who proved the rule – but consider the others – Wordsworth, for instance, or Milton – who never joked, never came down from their exalted levels except when they fell into a pit of bathos only possible for one with no sense of humour. There was a flicker of firelight: nearby a dog barked sharply and then was quiet: London was still for a moment: then the talk turned again.

The other memory is even more subjective. Once she asked me if I should like to see a poem she had just finished. Of course I would – please – but for a moment I was shaken by fear that I might not like it and feel wretchedly unable to say anything. It was 'But for Lust', still in her round, orderly, clear hand, not yet passed through the old-fashioned type-writer she uses so accurately. It startled and stirred me. No one else, I believe, had then seen it. For a moment she obviously thought my reaction fulsome: then, simply, that I had over-estimated the poem. No, it had not been sent to any periodical, and she did not know if or when it would be printed. Although I was neither editor nor publisher I asked, insistently, to be allowed to have it printed: and she let me take away a copy. War-time restrictions made the result physically meagre, a small, single fold in a cream card cover bearing the title: but the printing was clear and sympathetic. Fifty copies were struck off and numbered and signed by the poet. One was duly sent to the British Museum and we shared the remainder, using them a little later as Christmas cards which evoked a quite remarkable response from those who received them. That remains my solitary excursion into publishing: I do not hope ever to improve upon it.

It has always seemed to me that, in the quality and subtlety of her technique, Ruth Pitter is a poet's poet. But it would also be true to say that she is a poet in character; not, by any means, the caricature, 'poetic' poet; but equally not the person one is surprised to find 'writes poetry'. She grew up in an atmosphere of poetry: she has read and, importantly, remembered and spoken poetry without affectation, effort or, indeed, anything but complete acceptance, since she was a child; now, in vigorous age, she can produce work as firm, as sharp and as fresh as ever:

> Older than the house, the southwest wails;
> And the strong new house, like a house in the old tales,
> Is nothing but desire and fear forming and dissolving,
> With the wind streaming, with the world revolving.

Her enjoyment of poetry has always been catholic, and she in unforcedly capable of seeing the merits in any writing, but quite unforgiving of technical slovenliness. Her own work, in any mood or manner, has always been distinguished by a sensitive, virtually infallible ear. Anyone whose range is as wide as the compassion of 'Elegy to Mary', the gaiety of 'Digdog', the tragic power of 'The Heart's Desire is Full of Sleep', the scope of 'Comet', the lapidary delicacy of 'A Trophy of Arms', the majestic simplicity of 'But for Lust', the completeness of 'Sweet Other Flesh', and the period quality of 'Resurgam', must be extremely gifted to maintain a consistently high standard. Ruth Pitter has done so partly because her poetry has never been hurried : she has always wanted the right word and has not been content with less. She is, too, a purist; quiet about her writing, without arrogance, belonging to no clique, content to write and to publish : when she has published the process is, for her, complete. She remains for me the poet of the cool voice, clear through a troubled time.

IN MYSTERY

John Betjeman

Ruth Pitter has put poetry first in her life ever since she was a small child in the eastern suburbs of London. She is clear, mysterious, devout and humorous. Generally she uses rhythm and rhyme, and she is always easy to understand. Her earlier poems were like someone being let out of the house, and not allowed to leave the back garden. These are her exquisite detailed descriptions of flowers and insects. Sometimes they are very funny, like her poem about 'The Weed' addressing her fellow weeds in a cockney accent, and urging the slugs to demolish the valuable plants. Later she personalized cats, in a less Gilbertian manner than T. S. Eliot's. But her latest poems go out of the garden to the fields and sky. They are meditations and visions, each contained in only a few stanzas. There is a strong sense in them of a vast and shining world outside that in which we live. They do not ignore the miseries of existence, but they are full of expectant delight. 'I think a real poem,' she writes 'however simple its immediate content, begins and ends in mystery.' She is right. This is the effect all her poems create.

A SUPERB CRAFTSMAN

Richard Church

Ruth Pitter is an English poet whose work has been over-
looked although she has been writing for half a century. The
rage for 'fashionable' verse and experiments in unintelligibility
has been responsible for that neglect. Few wanted to read
work that was so quiet, so austere, so honest in its acknow-
ledgment of its sources.

One or two people, however, noticed Ruth Pitter at the beginning of her career as a poet. I remember that I was introduced to her work thirty-nine years ago by Hilaire Belloc,
one day at luncheon at The Gourmet, in Lisle Street. He told
me that he had just written a preface to a book of poems by
'a young woman who knew the meaning of literary discipline
and form'.

I got the book, was entranced by the deliberate manipula-
tion of syllables containing a passion of mood and reflection,
and something strangely humorous as well. I wrote an en-
thusiastic letter in the *Spectator*. Some years later I met the
author, and she said: 'Young man, you were good enough
to write about me somewhere or other'. I am five years her
senior.

She has not been a frequent visitor to her publishers. That
implies much self-criticism. Four years after that first intro-

duction, she produced a most odd little collection called A *Mad
Lady's Garland*, again with a preface by Belloc. Once more
the technical excellence commanded attention. Like Aesop
and La Fontaine, she spoke in this book through the mouths
of such minor critics of humanity as the flea, the spider, the
caterpillar, the domestic cat, the mayfly and the earwig. Des-
pairing of the direct approach to her goal, she attacked it by
this oblique method. The reprinting of these poems today, in
her first comprehensive collection, should gain a wide hear-
ing in a world which demands always more and more
novelty.

The most remarkable thing about her work is the sanity of
her judgment. She is not shaken by the latest craze. Like her
Virtuous Female Spider:

> I look not here for my reward,
> But recompense shall come
> When from this toilsome life and hard
> I seek a heavenly home;
> Where in the mansions of the blest,
> By earthly ills unmarred,
> I'll meet again my Love, my best
> And sole desired reward.

She has a remarkable ability to use ancient phrases, measures
and verse forms, and to imbue them with new life. She is
obviously a devoted student of Edmund Spenser. One might
say that her devices of using deliberate archaisms and inversions are copied from him, since he was the first English poet
to be so conscious of the historical development of his native
tongue as to be able to hark back to words and modes of
speech long fallen into disuse. She has also learned from
Spenser how to manipulate and digest a single idea so that it
can be perfectly contained within the limits of a single stanza.
Here is an example, which shows also her wholly humorous
resuscitation of obsolete phrases. The stanza, significantly a
Spenserian stanza, is from a poem called 'Resurgam' in which

a heretical caterpillar tells the bewildering story of his meta-
morphosis. He says:

> Methought I saw a wingèd creature fly
> That seemed most nearly of the Cherubim:
> His pinions white with many a dusky eye
> And dainty down on every part of him;
> Noble he was in every lightsome limb;
> He scorned to browse upon the herbage dun,
> But of the flowers which in his light were dim
> Sipped wantonly and tasted one by one;
> Then at my side sat down and glistered in the sun.

Notice the harmonious construction of the phrases, with
skilled delicacy of alliteration and round chiming of vowels
up and down the scale.

Now, in majestic contrast, listen to 'One Right Kind of
Music', published over thirty years later:

> It sings in the sun, sings in no valley below;
> Melts metal, hard mind, in fire, melts with no tear;
> Pants with no sigh, but sobs as the furnace sobs
> In its phoenix-throe. There cherub-burning the eye
> The insupportable eye of the furnace glares,
> Outfaces, beats down, prevails, looks through and
>   over,
> With the upward torrent of flame intent on fusion
> Devouring, adoring, roaring its tyrannous praise.
>
> Seeing what that heat sees is not to my mind.
> All dew is dried, all lily and nightingale
> Dismissed with a hiss. And yet, and yet, some bird
> Carols within that fire; warbling it woos,
> Like the three children walks warbling in flame;
> Nests in the flame, in the flux that abolishes me.

Here is the work of a superb craftsman who has laboured
long to know her craft – not in the verbally dandified steps

of Gerard Manley Hopkins, but by her own gestures of dogged spiritual exploration. That is why I believe her work will endure for a long time. It is non-fashionable, like all permanent things such as bread, and water, and a well-made kitchen table.

DEBONAIR

Robert Conquest

'Kind Ruth Pitter' as she understandably calls herself in 'The Frog and the Well', has that quality to be found in the old usage of the word debonair – with its ethical overtones. But, as it also perhaps implies, she gives us as well wit in the metaphysical sense – the controlled and moving elaboration of an image: 'The Beautiful Negress' is a perfect example.

She can also enter the realm of awe. The religious poem 'The Great and Terrible Dream' is one of those visions (like, though more personal and direct, Victor Hugo's 'La Trompette de Jugement') in the mood of apocalyptic nightmare. But her discovery that Christ is more terrible than death, because He and not it is invincible, takes us into spheres beyond Hugo's rather mechanical abyss.

As Roy Fuller says in his poem 'Dedicatory Epistle' – 'truth's half feeling and half style.' Though on the face of it Ruth Pitter's technical variety is not overwhelming, if we look more carefully we see it is something more. Drawing on the styles and feelings of the great discoveries of the past – whether seventeenth, eighteenth or nineteenth centuries – she makes them her own. At a time when it is sometimes thought to be a virtue to write as though the past did not exist, she shows it as a full component of the poetic present. As with Thomas

Hardy, though they are very different poets, the occasional archaism which might jar (as an artificiality almost as deplorable as eccentric neologism) is simply an odd but natural knot on a living tree.

Ruth Pitter has always shown an individuality of language. Often enough nowadays, eccentricity is thought to be an adequate substitute; it is not. For it remains, in the strictest sense, superficial, while the tone conveying the full depth of a real individual, in judgment and in feeling alike, is what we find in Miss Pitter: that is, the much misused word *style* – in its fullest meaning.

Ruth Pitter's reputation among people who are really concerned with poetry, rather than with just one more medium for expressing temporary fads, is of the highest. These few lines are no more than an expression of thanks for that particular pleasure; and a rare one it is.

LATTER PITTER

Roy Fuller

Ruth Pitter's is obviously a poetry of constant development; but more than that, it emerged from dauntingly restrictive bonds. The truly abysmal tradition she inherited is shown not so much by her own early work as by the prefaces written for it by Hilaire Belloc and James Stephens – generous and well-intentioned no doubt, but with scarcely a concrete word about poetry's standards and objects, and how far Miss Pitter's had achieved them. The purpose of those pieces by those then eminent littérateurs – they introduced volumes published by Miss Pitter in 1927, 1934, and 1936 – was obviously to call attention to a poet in danger of neglect in a changing and finally transformed poetic world. It was her misfortune (as I think) to have been born in 1897 with a talent so precocious that by the time the Eliot-Pound revolution had made itself felt, her poetic ways seemed set – ways of literary language, of abstraction, of traditional forms that imposed themselves upon rather than served the poet's individuality.

However, looking back one can see that Miss Pitter never really quite fitted into the Georgian tradition that survived, like some particularly pointless vestigial organ, throughout the twenties and thirties. Much of her work during the latter decade, for example, is so elaborate and parodic as to indicate

a kind of frustration of poetic impulse, though probably by
no means fully conscious. But it seems to me that not until
the collection of 1945, *The Bridge*, does she speak systematic-
ally in anything like a true voice – observation and thought
without the glaze of false 'poetry'. The precise is still on the
whole subservient to the worked-up general; but when it
appears it appears with great force, as in this stanza from
'Vision of the Cuckoo':

> Secure you walk, picking your food under the roses.
> The light on the large head is blue,
> The wings are netted cinnamon and umber,
> The soft dark eye is earthward, the silver belly
> Gleams with reflected pink from fallen petals.

Also new, I think, is the slangy or comic used for serious
purpose – for example, the line 'The sham harp with its
tinsel string allusively bust' in the poem 'Funeral Wreaths'.
And one feels that the essential optimism of outlook, having
weighed the worst, is fully earned: see 'Lament for Oneself'.
Perhaps the most remarkable poem in this book is 'The Bat',
but even here we still sense the struggle of marvellous observation and discriminating emotion against the various exigen-
cies of its couplets, its occasional echo of a mannered literary
mode.

In the two subsequent collections of new poems, *The Ermine*
(1953) and *Still by Choice* (1966) one does not find the variety
and realism that distinguished *The Bridge*. Miss Pitter did not
move closer to a language and technique that would have
enabled her to extend her range and speak more directly of
experience – but then the public events were over that lay
behind the poetry of *The Bridge*. And in compensation this
post-war work, particularly *Still by Choice*, gives one a pretty
constant sense of a poet with something important to say, a
characteristic rare at any time and elusive indeed during the
last twenty-odd years. Though not without disappointments,
the reader turns these pages always expecting to come upon

an urgent message. I would instance 'A Dream' as one of the poet's most successful raids on the incommunicable, but it is by no means an isolated success. And I would direct anyone in doubt of Miss Pitter's achievement to 'Night Flower Piece' and 'Exercise in the Pathetic Fallacy': poems like these must surely figure in any account of the century's verse. As a practitioner one can have nothing but admiration for a set of terza rima stanzas (the latter poem) that begins by posing this sort of technical and intellectual difficulty:

> This growing spiral snail of a gold colour
> Makes on flat liquid whiteness one event.
> There are three others. Pensive without dolour
>
> The citron sac he clings to, sacrament,
> Holds nothing in its unripe-lemon lumen
> But pure pale colour like an empty tent.

If only (one thinks) Miss Pitter had been born into a tradition less rigid, less established – if she had been American! Then the earlier years would almost certainly not have been – I won't say 'wasted' for no time is wasted in the arts which is devoted to disciplined expression – spent in trying to refurbish an heirloom hopelessly outdated and inutile. In skill, brain-power and sensibility she seems to me to compare with Marianne Moore and Elizabeth Bishop, but the older American was able to help make a mode of poetry apt to express the contemporary experience, and the younger to inherit it: neither had to struggle out of a dead chrysalis.

It may seem harsh to prognosticate that posterity will judge Ruth Pitter on the evidence of a comparatively few late poems, but then not many poets leave anything at all to posterity.

THE STRAWBERRY TRAY

Joyce Grenfell

It was just after the war, a time of grey austerity and inadequate heating, when I was asked to choose and read a programme of poetry on the wireless. As I remember, the idea was to do portraits in poetry and these were mostly portraits of people. I had a portrait of spring time from 'Love in a Valley'; and I had recently discovered Ruth Pitter's poem 'The Strawberry Plant' and I knew I had to include that, too.

So, wearing layers of wool against the cold, I paced the tiny area of the living-room reading aloud in the half-furnished flat we'd finally taken, in desperation, after weeks of searching in those difficult days. I was practising, in full voice, because it was a very noisy flat, high above a bus stop in the Kings Road. Even with the windows shut the Strawberry poem had to be spoken loudly although it is, I am sure, meant to be spoken low, for it is a quiet poem; a long quiet look at the exquisite 'odorous vermilion ball, tight with completion' with 'one greenish berry spangling into yellow where the light touched the seed', the whole set 'Above the water, in her rocky niche'.

I hadn't done much poetry reading at that time and I hoped to do justice to the poets I had chosen, so the chill air of the flat reverberated with words. (I am a dedicated practiser.)

The day after the broadcast I came home to find a small brown parcel had been delivered, by hand. Handwriting can give me as much pleasure as a satisfying drawing, or a poem. When writing sits firm on the paper it makes a true design. When it seems to hover it has no appeal to my eye. I cannot now remember exactly what the writing was like on that small parcel but I know it sat firm on the paper and I was drawn to it. Inside the wrapping was a small thick Gentleman's Relish-like pot, and painted on the lid was an enchanting portrait of a wild strawberry plant, fruit and flower, both out at once as so often happens in early June; and all was ceremoniously tied up with a gay blue ribbon with dancing ends. Ruth Pitter had heard the broadcast and the little painted pot was her thank you for it.

Few presents can have given anyone more pleasure than this gave me. The thing was a joy to behold. I very much admired the poet, and her gesture was a surprise of the happiest kind. I was truly delighted, showed off my treasure to all my available friends and wrote off at once to an address nearby, in Chelsea, to say thank you as positively as I knew how. Enthusiasm on paper can so easily look like gush and I could only hope that what I felt came up off the paper as I had put it down – with genuine warmth.

Then one day, standing in a queue, we met and I was able to tell Ruth Pitter what the strawberry pot meant to me. I asked her if she did much of that kind of thing and she told me she painted trays. I asked her if I could order one and, please, could it have a design of wild strawberries on it. She said she didn't often take special orders but she would see what she could do; did I want the background to be cream or black? I chose black.

I use my tray every day. It is one of our most precious possessions and we always have coffee on it after dinner and I also use it when people come to tea. It has a wreath of wild strawberries all around its oval shape and there is a small blue butterfly poised over a white strawberry flower. If you look very carefully you can find the mayfly hovering there, too. Constant use of the tray has marked it a little, even though I obey orders and clean it, as instructed on the typed card that came with it. This begins: 'Do not fear to use' and I certainly haven't. I do 'occasionally polish with a little ordinary paraffin finishing with a soft cloth'. Miss Pitter advises 'preferably silk' but I never seem to have any silk of worthy quality; an old fine linen handkerchief does very well instead.

My strawberry tray was the first Pitter tray I ever saw, but since then I have seen many for we have given some to special friends of all ages and we know that the ones still in England are in constant use, for we see them when we go out to tea or dinner. There are three, I know, in America, and one in Australia. These are mostly patterned in spring flowers with an occasional strawberry tucked into the garland. And one friend has a tray bright with a wreath of vegetables: little carrots, beetroots, peas, and spring onions. As far as I know mine is the only *all* strawberry tray and I am very honoured to be in possession of such a unique and pretty object.

I admire Ruth Pitter, both as a Christian and as a poet. I delight in her painting and if I had the talent I would play her my thanks in a whole programme of appreciation on the 'harp, dulcimer, lute, cymbal, trump and timbal, *and* the ever soothing flute'.

Instead I must just say my thanks for all the pleasure she has given me, and when I have typed the last word I will lift the lid of the cherished Gentleman's Relish pot that lives on my bedside table and take out a paper clip from it and pin these pages together to add to the rest of this book.

SMALL THINGS

Mary Grieve

The delicate expression of deep feeling is one of the great charms of Ruth Pitter's poetry and conversation. But I still knew only her poetry the day we met in a country town hotel to explore, hesitantly on both sides, the possibility of her writing a regular weekly article for the nine million readership of the weekly magazine Woman.

I had had no previous experience of offering to a poet of great distinction the means of communication with a mass. I did not know how she would accept the idea, I did not know how I would carry it through; or whether the whole project was one of those that should never have been taken beyond the first incautious, exciting attraction. But as we talked and saw each other's anxieties I felt that we were both ready to try our best and see what came of it. What we settled upon was that Ruth would write a weekly article on country ways and experiences, and that she would bring her religious beliefs into her articles as and when she wished.

The popular Press has long received with hospitality and noticeable nonchalance the writings of popular (preferably Low Church) parsons. But a poet – suffering the further oddness of being, in fact, a poetess – might indeed find it difficult to catch the affection of the millions whose experience of poetry probably did not extend to Palgrave.

But Ruth has the marvellous gift of bringing great and overwhelming messages through very small doors – for example, 'The Sparrow's Skull', which bears the sub-title: 'Memento Mori. Written at the Fall of France':

> The kingdoms fall in sequence, like the waves on the
>   shore.
> All save divine and desperate hopes go down, they are
>   no more.
> Solitary is our place, the castle in the sea,
> And I muse on those I have loved, and on those who
>   have loved me.
>
> I gather up my loves, and keep them all warm,
> While above our heads blows the bitter storm:
> The blessed natural loves, of life-supporting flame,
> And those whose name is Wonder, which have no
>   other name.
>
> The skull is in my hand, the minute cup of bone,
> And I remember her, the tame, the loving one,
> Who came in at the window, and seemed to have a
>   mind
> More towards sorrowful man than to those of her
>   own kind.
>
> She came for a long time, but at length she grew old;
> And on her death-day she came, so feeble and so bold;
> And all day, as if knowing what the day would bring,
> She waited by the window, with her head beneath her
>   wing.
>
> And I will keep her skull, for in the hollow here
> Lodged the minute brain that had outgrown a fear;

Transcended an old terror, and found a new love,
And entered a strange life, a world it was not of.

Even so, dread God! even so, my Lord!
The fire is at my feet, and at my breast the sword:
And I must gather up my soul, and clap my wings,
    and flee
Into the heart of terror, to find myself in thee.

There the minute skull, recalling the minute personality of
the sparrow, takes its place easily between a vast war and a
transcendent spiritual vision.

Her pleasure is often in small things; her revelation to us
is in her minute observation – in her poetry as in her flower
paintings. I remembered a line often quoted to me in my
home: 'I come in small things, saith the Lord.'

So we started—and week after week Ruth revealed the small
and the tender to an age hypnotised by the large, the noisy
and the brash. This, for instance, on fungi observed in Janu-
ary:

> One kind – I daresay you've seen it – is like a mass of
> gray velvet flounces with rich, soft ivory edges. It looks
> unbelievably expensive, like the trimmings of a Court dress
> for some elderly empress, especially when the dew is spark-
> ling on it, just like diamante.

Then, contemplating the variety of lichen:

> I wonder why God made such an endless variety of
> living things. The world is full of them: thousands and
> thousands of different forms of life. We often behave as if
> we were the only kind.

And here is a childhood memory, recalled with all the clarity,
feeling and economy of a master painter of the past:

> The firelight shone on the simple tea-things, and made
> the little low room all warm and glowing, with father,
> mother and children all happy to be there and happy to be

together. Outside a dull crimson sun sank down behind the cold, mysterious, purple woods, and an owl cried desolately over the drifted banks of snow that were already crackling with frost again.

One looks down a long perspective into that radiant scene, and somewhere out of one's own past come memories to match it.

Frugality and thrift were necessary disciplines in Ruth's childhood, but I think they became life-long companions by choice. In these domestic writings her satisfaction in good, economical husbandry and housewifery is abundantly expressed. The place she gives to her home-baked bread and well-made marrow-bed is important, unskimped. One believes that Ruth's disinterest in the time-saving gadgets of today springs not from their prohibitive price, but from the fact that she does not begrudge time spent on honest toil. Although Ruth disclaims attraction to the beliefs of Teilhard de Chardin, she synthesises the material and the spiritual in her own life and writing to a point which invites comparison.

She lives, and very often expresses herself, in the small and home-centred elements of being. Yet even when her scope is domestic, I believe she needs freedom of thought and movement – though she is seldom heard sighing for the Andes.

Ruth was seriously ill for some months in her late sixties; she says that through that painful experience she acquired greater power of acceptance and of self-discipline. Included in this is a calm and steady gaze on lessening strength and increasing dependence. She could show out of her own experience, and by her skill as a poet, how human beings have to face that testing time – the time of the diminishments. She who knows so well how hard it is 'to go at another's nod', could firm our step.

Ruth went through the experiences of her illness with something near zest – strange bedfellow for acute suffering. And she brought away enhanced discipline and comprehension. When she spoke to me some time later of the effects of severe illness and drugs she might have been talking of the excellent effects on her garden of digging and manuring and cutting deep into her soil. So in her hospital bed fruits were cultivated which are still hers today.

Leafing through the copies of Woman in which her series of articles were published I find this to record at the end of these recollections:

> There's a part of us that is always young, always hopeful . . . that only needs some little encouragement, like a fine day or a little kindness, to blossom into joy. It's our soul, I believe. It's always young simply because it's deathless, and it's always ready to blossom simply because its nature is delightful, in spite of its faults.
>
> The soul remembers. At least it seems like remembering. There are times when a great joy comes into it. This joy is so compelling and can seem so foreign to our nature, that we are often amazed at it. It seems to speak of a perfect bliss, of losing ourselves in the love of God.
>
> For a brief moment we are really and truly at home.

I wonder if ever the predicament, the ambivalence of naked apes has been presented so simply to so many. I wonder how many of those who read it ten years ago still hear an echo.

URANIA AS POET

Thom Gunn

To call Ruth Pitter a descriptive poet, or a nature poet, is misleading in that it implies limitations that are not hers. It is more fruitful and more accurate to point out that she is a poet who works primarily through the senses. Yet even this statement needs to be explained to do justice to her subtlety.

Like many poets, her first recourse is to accurate evocation of physical detail. The simplest of her details are of this sort:

> Drifting grape-coloured shadows on the hill,

or

> When in the oozy water-nooks
> The muffling cresses hush the brooks.

Vivid as these perceptions are, we do not need the give-away of 'oozy' to detect an echo of Keats. But Keats was only a start for her. Something much more sophisticated is going on when she describes a strawberry as 'tight with completion'. She *seems* to be merely continuing her description of the strawberry, but in doing so she is actually saying a lot of other things, that the strawberry's 'tightness' precedes its disintegration, that ripens is also a step toward death. Similarly, when she says

The fleeting eye-beam from the dying eye
Plunges into the abysses of the sky
Where the vast roses of creation die,

the image of the last line is more than merely physical detail,
though it is certainly that among other things. The dying
galaxies are like roses because roses are transitory as well as
beautiful, because they expand as they die. The comparison
is not illustrative, it is the whole point: the sensuous apprehension has in fact triggered the intellectual. And the quietness with which she performs this complicated feat is
characteristic: Ruth Pitter is the most modest of poets, slip-
ping us her riches as if they were everyday currency.

Something rather similar happens on a larger scale in
whole poems. One's first impression is that she is a simple,
almost a naïve, poet, and it is an impression that she
encourages. It is usually completely false. 'The Ermine' is
typical of the way she works. It looks at first sight like a
poem for children. And in it she claims a blundering character,
that of 'rough-handed homespun.' (Similarly the subtle
Chaucer would pretend naïveté.)

I know this Ermine. He is small,
Keen-biting, very quick withal.
He dies of soil. He is the snow.

But the opposition of black soil and white snow thus easily
set up becomes very complex after a few lines.

Royal he is. What makes him so?
Why, that too is a thing I know:
It is his blame, his black, his blot;
The badge of kings, the sable spot.
O subtle, royal Ermine, tell
Me how to wear my black as well.

The simple antitheses – soil and snow, black and white,
animal and human being – have melted into the real, into
the mixed unsimple world itself.

64

The thing-in-the-world contains its own complexity. Words can operate in two ways at once: they can present it to us in all its sensuously-apprehended reality and they can simultaneously explore its ambiguity. There are many other poems where she performs this difficult double action, carrying us with her through her clear vision to her clear understanding. One of the best is 'Urania':

> Winter and night, the white frost and the darkness
> fall, and the hands of life release the spirit;
> gladly she goes hence to her starry pasture.
>
> Frostbound, the plough leans idle on the headland;
> now the benighted hind forsakes the furrow;
> earth is at peace, no longer vexed with labour.
>
> With still delight the soul receives the omen,
> thinks on her travail in the sowing season,
> calmly remembers all the heat of harvest:
>
> knows that the end is fairest; sees the heavens
> hung with creation: in the woody valley
> sees on the earth one star that steals towards her.
>
> It is Urania: through the darkened woodland
> now she advances: now she brings her vestal
> lamp to the tomb, with nameless consolation.

Winter, it turns out, is a time when creation is not ended but suspended, for, while 'frostbound, the plough leans idle on the headland', we see 'the heavens hung with creation'. The cold is a time when images appear at their sharpest, and thus, paradoxically, in all their potential for richness. Urania the goddess is both fertile and vestal. Her name is not only that of this poem but also that of a selection from Ruth Pitter's work published some years ago; and she is indeed an appropriate image for the poetry itself, which too is fertile and vestal.

POET OF MANY MOODS

L. P. Hartley

I am honoured to be asked to contribute my word of praise to Miss Ruth Pitter. She is in the direct tradition of English poetry: her poems are lyrical, beautiful, intellectual, and emotional. They present few conundrums and no teasing, brain-scraping images; they are pure poetry, not ingenious collocations of words.

Her 1966 volume *Still by Choice* has all the quality of her earlier work. It appeals to the heart and to the mind, and it has the poet's ability to convey in words the effect of music. Her range of interest and sympathy is wide, and it extends equally to Nature and to human nature.

She can write poems that are closely-worked, carved like gems, and immediately intelligible, and others that are wayward and impressionistic, leaving much to the imagination. Indeed, her meanings are seldom enclosed within the mere meanings of her words.

She is a poet of many moods, and of many responses to those moods; and she has an original and exciting mastery over words. It is difficult to say she is a poet of this sort or of that. Her gift is eclectic; she has no besetting theme, no besetting style. The wind bloweth where it listeth, and her inspiration is as various and unpredictable as the wind is. But

66

whatever she sees and hears and thinks and feels, she translates into poetry that has the freshness of the seasons, and the power of multifold revival that is inherent in the heart of man.

HERSELF

Elizabeth Jennings

Ruth Pitter is a poet who has never been associated or aligned with literary groups or movements; her finest work is her own entirely, seeming to have few forbears or influences. It is a poetry of nature and of religious utterance, but it speaks always with a complete originality and freshness.

In her last book, *Still By Choice*, she writes with a new, surprising strength:

> Some beat the glass as if in agony,
> The pattern never still enough to see;
> In the unearthly strong cold radiance
> Eyes glitter, wings are flourished, weapons glance,
> Furs, metals, dyes; duellers with flashing foils
> Glitter like fire and struggle in the toils
> Of potent light, as deep-sea fish are drawn
> From profound dark to anguish and the dawn.

That stanza, from 'Moths and Mercury-Vapour Lamp', shows Ruth Pitter at her most powerful; each word is carefully selected and, from a moderate and calm beginning, she builds up to effects of great strength and emotion.

She resists labels. She is herself – that is all one can say. Although there sometimes seems to be a too cloistered air about her work, this judgment is rapidly altered by poems of power and passion. She is a poet who stands on no ceremony, strikes no attitudes. There is one particular charge one could never lay against Ruth Pitter. She never, for an instant, appears to be either a 'poetess' or a 'prophetess', with all that those words apply in denigration. She is a quiet poet, certainly, but one whom one can return to again and again and find renewed pleasure. Some of her work seems surely to be of permanent value.

PROUD TRIBUTE

P. J. Kavanagh

We are all neglected poets.

Some because we neglect the poet inside us, others because we try not to be neglectful, we even write poems, but nobody listens. Even if they do listen and make a fuss of us there is no such thing as a successful poet – except perhaps for a brief moment at the completion of a poem – if a poem is ever truly completed.

The best we can do, if we are very lucky and very good, or very wicked in the right, difficult way, is to be true to ourselves and the poem, both. Ruth Pitter has done this which is why she is worth saluting.

There is in her poems the gnat-cry that is inside all good poems and which speaks for all of us. (All, that is, except those too horrible to count.) It is quiet but it is clear and unscared. It may be that in years to come our anthologies will empty of the loud and she will be heard. It may be that loudness is a factor in dealing with the deaf. (Poets are deaf too.) It doesn't matter. She has said what she had it in her to say. And if I think that is a proud tribute it is because if anyone in similar circumstances were to pay it to me I know I would smile to myself for the first time for years. Or burst into tears. Or both.

'Time's fool but not heaven's: yet hope not for any return.'

RUTH PITTER'S HUMBLER CREATION

James Kirkup

> O *measureless* Might, *ineffable* Love!
> While *angels delight to hymn Thee above,*
> The *humbler creation, though feeble their lays,*
> With *true adoration shall lisp to thy praise.*

Hymns Ancient and Modern.

English poetry has always had a peculiar sympathy for animals, birds, fish and insects. Among the many great poems about 'the humbler creation', my own preferences are for those by Herrick, Clare, Smart and Blake; for the works of the Japanese *haiku* poets, particularly Issa; and, among the moderns, above all for Lawrence, with his extraordinary gift for entering into the skin and the soul of creatures as various as mosquitoes, kangaroos and tortoises. I do not care for Eliot's insufferable cats; but I like Theodore Roethke's flora and fauna (his sloth!), Ted Hughes' brilliant beasts, Marianne Moore's personal zoo (and her fabulous La Fontaine), the legendary and domestic denizens of the jolly jungle of Stevie Smith, and Elizabeth Bishop's roosters.

Ruth Pitter belongs to these happy few, a Society for the

Invention of Poetry about Animals (SIPA). But her world is not the world of societies; it is a world of mostly very small, dun-coloured creatures living in pain, solitude, discomfort, gentleness and visionary grief. Theirs is the true world, not the banal world we see around us every day.

She has always seemed to me a direct descendant of Blake and Clare, with some of the luminous mysticism of Vaughan. Blake's tiger is there in her work, but more often it is his lamb, his redbreast, his fly. Her animal and bird subjects (in this essay I shall not refer to her witty, serious light verse) include such magnificent creatures as swans, ermines, foxes, ptarmigans, a bird of paradise, a caged lion and a glorious tigress:

> The raging and the ravenous,
> The nocturnal terror in gold,
> Red-fire-coated, green-fire-eyed,
> The fanged, the clawed, the frightful leaper,
> Great-sinewed, silent walker,
> Tyrant of all the timid, the implacable
> Devil of slaughter, the she-demon
> Matchless in fury, matchless love
> Gives her whelps in the wildernesses.

(As an example of 'Polymorph Pervers', it is interesting to compare this poem with a poem about a gorgeous human being, 'The Beautiful Negress', which I feel sure is a portrait of a splendid African woman who was for some years my landlady in a rooming house over Goodge Street Station.

> ... O solemn Beauty, when upon my way
> You walked in majesty, did not the tear
> Leap up to crown you with more light than day?
> Did not the silent voice within the ear
> Cry Fly with her to the soul's Africa,
> Night, tragedy, the veiled, the end prefer?

This poem gives to a T my dear old friend, Madame Sheba, with her tall, massive upright figure crowned by an intri-

cately-wreathed turban, as she used to sweep along Totten-
ham Court Road, carrying all before, and behind, her, in those
glum post-war London days. Madame Sheba had the same
matchless fury, matchless love, that are in the tigress.)

Then there is the heavenly lion in the second section of
'My God Beholds Me', a section subtitled 'The Lion-seraph':

> To love the Lion I will dare;
> He waves in heaven his flames of hair:
> Comet of beauty, through each limb
> The entire being informeth him . . .

But it is in the poems about the truly 'humble' inhabitants
of the animal kingdom that the most exquisite part of Ruth
Pitter's poetic sensibility is expressed. In these poems she
reveals herself most clearly as the 'poet of purity', which is
what Rudolph Gilbert calls her in his study, *Four Living
Poets*.* I feel her own rare personality shining and quivering
in her apprehensions of modest beings like sparrows, crows,
stockdoves, hoverflies, spiders, snails and hens. They are seen,
sharply and poignantly, against backgrounds of orchards,
weeds, woods, churchyards, brooks and meadows. Their colours
are humble, too, as she says in a wonderful evocation of
natural tones, 'Dun-colour':

> Subtle almost beyond thought are these dim colours,
> The mixed, the all-including, the pervasive,
> Earth's own delightful livery, banqueting
> The eye with dimness that includes all brightness . . .
> . . . For the rose-duns, and the blue-duns, look to the
> finches:
> For the clear clear brown-duns, to the fallow deer
> (How the sudden tear smarts in the eye wearied of
> cities)
> And for all these and more to the many toadstools,
> Which alone have the violet-dun, livid yet lovely:

* Rudolph Gilbert. *Four Living Poets*. Unicorn Press: Santa Barbara,
California, 1944.

But the most delicate duns are seen in the gentle
Monkeys from the great forests, the silvan spirits:
Wonderful! that these, almost our brothers,
Should be dressed so rarely, in sulphurous-dun and
    greenish;
O that a man had grassy hair like these dryads!
O that I too were attired in such dun-colours!

In this aspect of her genius she continues the unique visionary love of creation that we find in Blake's 'The Fly', the poem
of Blake's that I think is most like her own work:

Little Fly,
Thy summer's play
My thoughtless hand
Has brush'd away.

Am not I
A fly like thee?
Or art not thou
A man like me?

For I dance,
And drink, and sing,
Till some blind hand
Shall brush my wing.

If thought is life
And strength and breath,
And the want
Of thought is death;

Then am I
A happy fly,
If I live
Or if I die.

This is where Blake, Pitter and the Japanese *haiku* poets
come together in a common concern, realistic, unsentimental

and sometimes visionary, for the little creatures who share this fleeting existence with us. Issa writes thus of a fly, with wry observation, giving us a message similar to Blake's:

> The fly is asking you
> To save his life
> By wringing his hands.

In the dazzling 'Hoverfly on Poppy', Ruth Pitter writes:

> Like a man reaping, on the mealy edge
> Of the blond Poppy's anther-ring he stands,
> Pressing his breast against the fecund hedge,
> And gathering the pollen as with hands;
> Glittering heroic on the gold and red
> He ravishes his bright Lethean bread . . .

Her beautiful poem, 'Stormcock in Elder', describes a broken-roofed little cottage glorified by the presence of a brilliant little singing bird in the elder tree overhanging it. Here a humble abode becomes a hermitage, a house of vision and humility, as in Issa's *haiku*:

> A few flies and I
> Keep house together
> In this humble home.

This always reminds me of Ruth Pitter's

> Whatever place is poor and small,
> The Hut was poorer still,
> Stuck, like a snail upon a wall,
> On what we called a hill . . .

Pitter usually exhibits the true *haiku* qualities of frugality, modesty, elegant economy that makes something of nothing, as Sora does in his poem about the butterfly:

> Up the barley rows,
> Stitching, stitching them together,
> A butterfly.

I have already mentioned what I must call her 'serious' light verse. The wit underneath all her work is the observant, unexpected sideways-glance of the *haiku* or the satirical *senryu*, as in Issa's

> The firefly darts and leaves
> Its light behind it –
> Out of breath.

Crows, owls, dandelions, morning glories, spiders and snails are all favourite subjects of *haiku* makers, and we find all these, and many other 'humble' themes, in Ruth Pitter's *Still by Choice* (1966):

> The spider and the snail,
> Nocturnal, self-enclosed and self-secreting,
> Close web and slimy trail,
> Work coldly in the pale
> Ghost-glimmer, co-existing but not meeting.

Her morning glory's face is described with the compactness and plainness of statement of a Japanese poet's intent vision, swift brush:

> With a pure colour there is little one can do:
> Of a pure thing there is little one can say.
> We are dumb in the face of that cold blush of blue,
> Called glory, and enigmatic as the face of day . . .

From the same book, I select at random two lines from 'Tawny Owl in Fir-Tree' which, divorced from the grave and tragic weight of the whole poem, show the sharp and fleeting likeness of an owl as we might encounter it in a *haiku* or a brush-painting:

> Loose tawny feathers like dishevelled hair
> Stir on her stony forehead in cold air . . .

It is in poems like 'The Bat' and 'The Bush-Baby' that Ruth Pitter shows her true love for her fellow-creatures. Her horror

of the bat turns to understanding and love when she takes it
in her hands:

> Even fear must yield to love,
> And pity makes the depths to move.
> Though sick with horror, I must stoop,
> Grasp it gently, take it up,
> And carry it, and place it where
> It could resume the twilight air.

> Strange revelation! warm as milk,
> Clean as a flower, smooth as silk!
> O what a piteous face appears,
> What great fine thin translucent ears!
> What chestnut down and crapy wings,
> Finer than any lady's things –
> And O a little one that clings!

And of the bush-baby:

> I would rather hold this creature in my hand
> Than be kissed by a great king.
> The love for what I do not understand
> Goes from me to the slight thing.

> The moth-velvet and the round nocturnal eyes
> And the unchanging face
> Are excellent as an image out of Paradise,
> As a flower in a dark place.

> There is only mutual inoffensiveness
> Between us, and a sense
> Here in my heart, of what it is to bless
> A simple immanence;

> To see a glory in another kind,
> To love, and not to know.

O if I could forsake this weary mind
And love my fellows so !

We can disregard the poet's conventional worry at the end
of that lovely little poem; people are after all not all that important, except in so far as they exhibit the qualities of
modesty, quietness, patience and innocence found in 'our
dumb friends'. Not so dumb as most humans gifted with un-
necessary speech !

To my mind, Ruth Pitter's noblest achievement has been
in making us conscious of this humbler creation, and in showing us how, by contemplating it and entering into it, we can
divest ourselves of our smug self-importance and self-righteous-
ness. Hers is a timeless art that will endure far beyond the
poetic follies and fads of those far from humble creatures, the
more vociferous poets of today.

THRALLDOM

Carolyn Kizer

I would love to be in the Festschrift for Ruth Pitter. It is a great pity that my old friend Theodore Roethke is no longer with us, as he worshipped her work, in fact introduced me to it. He in turn first heard of her poetry through Stanley Kunitz, who later wrote about her most beautifully in the issue of my magazine *Poetry Northwest*, which was devoted to her work in 1960. To quote from our editorial on that occasion:

'The work of Ruth Pitter may not be widely known in America, but it is deeply known. Those who are familiar with her work will never shake off the thralldom of those cool, sensuous, melancholy, perfectly disciplined, frequently ecstatic poems:

'And again think on bright hair
That was yellow, before it became dust,
As broom looketh that blows in the upland air,
But never think upon the hearts of the just . . .

'This is a fragment from 1918. Thirty years later, the archaisms are muted, but we hear the chiming of that unmistakeable voice:

'. . . man and beast die, fall and go,
Under the sky's pall, rain or snow . . .

'It is surely the greatest privilege that we as editors will have, that Miss Pitter has entrusted to this small new magazine her unpublished poems of the past six or seven years, as well as allowing us to use a selection of poems from *The Ermine* which have not appeared in the United States. So, by her grace, this issue of *Poetry Northwest* commends itself to posterity. If life persist, and literature endure, so shall these pages.

'Then Alleluia all my gashes cry;
My woe springs up and flourishes from the tomb
In her lord's likeness, terrible and fair,
Knowing her root, her blossom in the sky . . .'

I AM FIDELITY

Stanley Kunitz*

'I am fidelity that still abideth.' More than thirty years have
gone since I first encountered that unexceptional, almost self-
effacing line in one of Ruth Pitter's early poems. I do not
know why it should persist in my mind, indelibly associated
with her name, but because it does, claiming no virtue beyond
its stubborn memorability, I begin to discover in it an inner
reality that has nothing to do with pious sentiment. I read
it anew as a kind of signature, an emanation.

In some ways she seems the loneliest poet of her generation, though marked by a self-reliant joy. From the first she
was precocious and irreconcilable. One of her perilous
triumphs is that she could have written as well as she did
without permitting herself, until middle life, to concede the
existence of the twentieth century. Conventional poesy and
piety were temptations she did not always escape; but out of
her dogged loyalty to traditional measures and archaic diction,
to Elizabethan song and Jacobean air, flowed some unrivalled
recreations.

Ruth Pitter became a modern poet without forfeiting her
right to deal with sacred experience. The natural world
remains miraculous to her. Her later poems are harder fought,

* This piece was first published in 1960. See p. 79.

less touched with innocence, but the best of them, however knowingly desolate, are still fortified by her sense of musical delight, her idiosyncratic purity of heart and eye. 'But for lust we could be friends . . .'

Her poems are so sensitively tuned that they are liable, with a breath, to fail, but even when they do they are never failures of conscience. I like to pick my way among her pieces, in that small Eden, half peaceable kingdom, half battleground, which is yet spacious enough for passion and betrayal, faith and its absence, cottage and cave, angel and military harpist, creatures of earth and air . . .

Praise to Ruth Pitter for having the morality to endure!

RARE BIRD

Naomi Lewis

A poet who writes, without weakness, for nearly half a century, in the main metrical stream, yet not unaware of changing tides; accomplished but not ornate nor quite predictable, keeping the reader alert throughout by a unique, individual voice – such a character is at no time frequent, and one who survives today is particularly worth attention. A fusion of time, dedication and circumstance make Ruth Pitter indeed a rare bird. This essay is an attempt to track down in her work the nature of this rarity: to capture the sound, if you like, of her original voice.

Should we decide that her place is with the English pastoral poets and leave it at that? It is a long, enduring, vigorous native line. Certainly her recurring personal themes of joy, grief, stillness, contemplation, frugality even, are most readily interpreted through the springs and winters, nights and mornings, birds, beasts, trees and hedge-flowers of an abiding rural landscape. Has she not described herself as one whose chief consolation has been 'the ineffable communion with the earth itself and some of its creatures?' Even more specifically – and more unusually – she has spoken of being most strongly moved by 'the mystery of life other than human, particularly the life of plants . . . They have speech without concepts . . . a strange mystical emanation, as of truth perceived in a vision or a dream.' Often, indeed, her gaze as grass or leaf or tree can have the illuminating directness that is always in Clare; it can also hold the poignant revelation that Edward Thomas could always strike from the sudden fused apprehension of, say, plant, time, rain, and a stilled implacable grief.

But the pastoral poem itself has never been as simple as it appears, not even in the medieval carollings of spring returned, or those sixteenth-century songs of May and daisied grass and the age-old, ever-young piping of shepherd boys. Even when children write verse of sunset or summer, the images are all too often arrived at through fancies already in the air, in song or print. And yet the experience of literature is as much a part of life as the experience of a new living place or a new love. Hints of Ruth Pitter's path through other poetry can be tracked through her own poetic work, like the white stones dropped in the forest that can lead the legendary traveller back to his own beginnings. So we can hear in her work the plucked-string plaint of the Elizabethan lyric, something of early Milton, of Smart and Darley perhaps, of Rossetti, Hardy, Meredith (surely), of Blunden too, and Blake unquestionably. But as with all of these in their time, the single poet's voice that comes out of it all is separate, new, and distinct.

It is fair to say that much (but how much?) of the exhilaration and surprise of this seemingly formal poetry comes from its statement, the curious paths of thought through which the reader is drawn. True, it is on the not unfamiliar themes of the day's response to the human journey. But don't expect the trampled surfaces and yearning sloughs of the usual emotional battlegrounds. Pitter-country lies rather further on, skirting or crossing those regions by routes of its own. A poem that holds a clue to it is 'The End of Fear' – best read a second time and a third for its real intent:

> When a man has cast out fear
> All is indifferent, and dear.

When desire has fled away
Then the little mice can play.

Leaning against the cedar's bark,
Or on a bear's neck in the dark,

Or lying in the mighty grass,
He is saved from what he was.

He can lay his head upon
Another's bosom, or a stone,

And the stone is well beloved,
And the breast by love unmoved:

The flesh uncursed and the stone blest,
The breast a stone, the stone a breast.

Or you can enter this place by way of that enigmatic poem 'The Task'. But 'Better than Love' is an even more striking example:

...Who can be what the weed was
In the empty afternoon?
Who can match me the wild grass,
Sighing its forgotten tune:
Who is equal to that shell,
Whose spiral is my parable?

No human eye reflects the weed
Burning beneath the lonely sun:
The wild hard grass spangled with seed
Is still unmatched by anyone:
The justice of the shell is still
Above the mind, above the will.

Since love and beauty, blown upon,
Are not desired, nor spoken of,
Hear me, you solitary one,
Better than beauty or than love,
Seen in the weed, the shell, the grass,
But never in my kind, alas!

The ragged weed is truth to me,
The poor grass honour, and the shell
Eternal justice, till I see
The spirit rive the roof of hell
With light enough to let me read
More than the grass, the shell, the weed.

Here is the kind of revelation that Clare arrived at by the intuitive flash of his earlier days, and later by the soaring leap of a mind no longer checked by reason. But the poem has a tense power of its own. 'The justice of the shell' – this is not only an image of hard perfection, but a key to the whole.

Silence and stillness: these are the insistent elements of this domain. For Ruth Pitter these are absolute experiences; indeed few poets have ever rendered the idea of silence with such intensity. Milton's temper often responded to it; yet his 'Silence was pleased' is a brilliant conceit. It seems to me that a few poems by Rossetti (Gabriel, not Christina whose passionate resignations have little in common with her) come nearest to her apprehension of silence and held time: notably 'The Woodspurge' and 'My Sister's Sleep'. But of all her poems evoking silence, those in the Sapphic metres that she occasionally uses are surely the most effective. Her celebrated 'Urania' (p. 65) is an evident example. But no less remarkable is 'Of Silence and the Air', a Sapphic poem describing, in her own words, 'a mystical experience on a winter night':

Here where the cold pure air is filled with darkness
graced but by Hesper and a comet streaming,

86

censed by the clean smoke from a herdsman's hearth-
stone
    I stand with silence:

void of desire, but full of contemplation
both of these herds and of the gods above them:
mindful of these, and offering submission
    to those immortal.

Older than they, the frosty air about me
speaks to the flocks like careful age, like winter,
saying, Seek shelter: to the gods, I know ye:
    and to me, nothing

save but that silence is the truth: the silent
stars affirm nothing, and the lovely comet
silent impending, like a nymph translated
    abides in heaven.

Shall I not also stand and worship silence
till the cold enter, and the heart, the housewife.
spin no more, but sit down silent in the presence
    of the eternal?

What this vision aspires to, and at moments seems to reach,
is caught in some verses of her extraordinary poem 'The
Eternal Image':

Standing so still, what does she see?
She sees the changeless creature shine
Apparelled in eternity:

She knows the constancy divine;
The whole of life sees harvested,
And frozen into crystalline

And final form, the quick, the dead,
All that has ever seemed to change,
Possess at once the pale and red:

All that from birth to death may range
Newborn and dead she sees, nor says
The vision to be sad or strange.

How may this serve her mortal ways?
Truly it cannot buy her bread
Nor ease the labour of her days:

But calm her waking, quiet her bed,
For she has seen the perfect round
That binds the infant to the dead,

And one by one draws underground
All men; and still, and one by one,
Into the air the living bound

Never completed, not begun . . .

A remarkable achievement. And yet it is fortunate, I think, that Ruth Pitter does not often explore this distance, too far removed from the provocative friction of daily detail.

But as even these few examples must clearly show, it is not ideas alone that make a poem. The impact of the form has always with her a particular potency; as we read, we cannot help remarking her verbal ease and the range of her technique. Her 'Lament for the Landless', for instance, with its rich language, its metrical interest, its precise yet intricate thought, would be a pleasantly challenging exercise for translation into other languages.

'I have tended', she has said, 'on the one hand to experiment, and on the other to strive towards an ideal of simplicity.' This simplicity, she adds, is best achieved 'when the syllabic metre happens to fit the ordinary speech rhythm without distortion, so that it might be a child speaking, and yet it is poetry.'

'The Mayfly', with its lovely, deceiving economy, offers one kind of simplicity:

> I the day's beauty am
> And the night's sorrow
> From the dark deep I came
> And go tomorrow.

A more significant instance is her poem 'Herding Lambs':

> In the spring, in the morning,
> We heard the high bleat,
> And the low voice of the ewes, and the rainlike
> Rustle of feet.
>
> In the daffodil day
> My sister called to me,
> And out to the garden gate
> We went to see.
>
> No dogs, no sticks,
> No shouting, no noise,
> Only the rustle, the bleating,
> The chirping boys.
>
> Slowly they moved along
> Herded by three
> Old grey men, and five children,
> To the fresh lea.
>
> And when a silly lamb
> Turned back in fright
> A withered or an infant hand
> Guided him right.

The early mist muffled their sound,
Muted that double chime
Trembling along the grassy ground
From the morning of time.

The force is of course in the final line, in which the vast import of 'morning', doubly used, only gradually breaks on us.

But this kind of simplicity is not her most frequent manner.

On the whole, I think, she prefers a coiled-spring tension, of a kind reaching back to the metaphysical seventeenth century. Nevertheless an observant eye or ear can find many other echoes. Her superb use of Sapphics has already been illustrated. 'Weeping Water, Leaping Fire' rings through the past from a sixteenth-century lyric source. In 'An Old Woman Speaks of the Moon' she catches the strange eluding plaintive Irish measure by which Thomas Moore continues to touch us to this day. Still more does she do this in 'The Military Harpist' – the most surprising poem, I suppose, in her collection.

But let us not lose sight of the original pursuit. Is there an end to the quest? I have said nothing so far of her animal poems – both the serious, beautiful poems on viper or bat or cygnet or hen or bees or dead bird ('May 1947') and the affectionate sets of verses on cats, engaging as they are. There are too her poems in a rustic, humorous vein, but I could more easily spare these than most. Lively as they are, I think that they divert us from the course. Is the true voice best found in 'The Military Harpist', which shows that her contemplation *can* be turned on to uncharacteristic themes?

Anthologists, who favour the short and the light, have not been the best of guides. Yet if I had to choose one piece whose tempo, style, scene and detail contain most fully what is her own, and her best, it might well be the leisured contemplative poem 'The Fishers', with its beautiful gliding sounds, held time, and absolute union of word and scene and

thought. Here are its opening and closing stanzas, though
it should be read *in toto*:

The embattled towers, the level lilied moat,
Between the lily-leaves the inverted sky,
The impending alders and the quivering float
Charmed the vexed spirit, and it was not I,
But contemplating essence that surveyed
The brightness, and the water, and the shade.

. . .

And the tall flower was peace made visible,
The air was ambient love; the flashing fly
Was the soul's dear mysterious parable,
Proclaiming the immortal silently;
And sweetest kindness sat beneath the trees
In two unasked, affectionate presences.

Good children, I am glad we made no kill;
That would have tarnished what I felt for you.
Two gentle souls, in whom was nothing ill,
Looked from the dark eye and the dreaming blue,
Where by the water and the tower of might
The hurt healed, and the mind was filled with light.

Peace made visible; ambient love; the mysterious and the
immortal . . . Best stop here. Why go further? Why indeed?
Though there are pastures enough if you have the wish to try.

WHEN SHE SPEAKS

Rupert Bruce Lockhart

The first time Ruth Pitter's name appeared on the Brains Trust, I turned on my television set in good time; for I was fired by my pre-war admiration of her poems, and determined not to miss a moment of this first sight of her. I was quite unprepared for the beauty of her speaking voice. I was thunderstruck: here was some of the magic of the voice of Ellen Terry, never forgotten since the first time I heard it in 1910.

For many years I have puzzled over what has happened to the female voice in England, especially in our theatre. All human voices are a balance between what in singing and voice production jargon we call 'chest' and 'head', sometimes known as 'thick' and 'thin'. For at least thirty years the voices of most English actresses (mercifully not quite all) have been afflicted by a horrifying over-balance, the chest voice falling right off its end of the seesaw. The result has been a breathy, superficial, high-pitched sound, presumably meant to convey an *ingénue* youthfulness.

This loss of the lower register took place at the time when critics and public began to complain bitterly of inaudibility in our theatre. How it arose is to me something of a mystery. Moreover, it is prevalent also among singers. In the singing world the chest voice in a woman is regarded with terror by the average teacher or student.

So I was enthralled when in the first sentence spoken by Ruth Pitter through my television set, I heard again the magic of Ellen Terry's spoken English. It was still more wonderful, later, to hear her speak her own poetry and quote the work of other poets. Here was the perfect coordination of chest and head exemplified by singers of the calibre of Destinn, Caruso and Kirkby Lunn – a coordination which I had almost thought extinct. Listen to Ruth Pitter speak of the Powers of Darkness, and Pluto himself appears before you.

It is, I believe, rare to hear a poet speak his own poetry in an exceptional voice. When one tells Ruth Pitter this, she modestly answers that she has the advantage of a strong physique. I think there is more to it than this; and how I wish she could impart her method of speaking to the young actresses of today.

The magic of Ellen Terry's voice has remained with me for over fifty years. Ruth Pitter's will remain for the rest of my life.

HER ANIMAL KINGDOM

Edward Lucie-Smith

Ruth Pitter's poems about animals are, like Andrew Young's, among her best and most characteristic. The reason is that they are both essentially metaphysical writers, and the links between the human and the animal kingdom come naturally to both of them. As Miss Pitter exclaims in her poem about 'The Bush Baby':

> To see a glory in another kind,
> To love, and not to know,
> O if I could forsake this weary mind
> And love my fellows so!

Technically, this stanza is typical – apparently conventional, yet brought to life by a very personal and sensitive awkwardness, the speaking tone which is never sacrificed to slickness of rhythm.

Though they spring from a unified sensibility, and are written in the same tone, it is possible to divide Miss Pitter's animal poems into two distinct categories, which in turn throw light on the poet's work taken as a whole. On the one hand, there are the ones which are deliberately emblematic: 'The Viper', for instance, or 'Caged Lion'. On the other, there are those which spring from some incident which the writer has actually seen and experienced, such as 'The Stockdove', 'The Swan Bathing', or 'The Crow'. I do not think I shall be alone in preferring the second kind. 'The Swan Bathing' is a beautiful poem because the observation is so precise, and the language which clothes it so limpid:

> . . . then as if fainting he falls sidelong,
> Prone, without shame, reveals the shiplike belly
> Tumbling reversed, with limp black paddles waving . . .

The detached, self-possessed, controlled tone is maintained until the trope which concludes the poem:

> . . . and one cold feather
> Drifts, and is taken gently by the rushes;
> By him forgotten, and by her remembered.

Perhaps strangely, this reminds me of the work of a very different poet, of a much younger generation – Ted Hughes. Hughes's tone has an underlying violence which is alien to Miss Pitter's work, but she shares his power to project himself into an animal existence. Hughes, for instance, speaks of the way the pike in a pond move

> . . . stunned by their own grandeur,
> Over a bed of emerald, silhouette
> Of submarine delicacy and horror.
> A hundred feet long in their world.

I do not think that there is any other literature besides our own which possesses so many fine lyrics about the animal kingdom. The birds and beasts of the Greek Anthology, whom Norman Douglas once described in a delightful book, are rivalled by those which English poets have captured in words. Among this company, Miss Pitter stands very high.

FROM GRATITUDE

Ngaio Marsh

I am grateful for being re-introduced to Ruth Pitter's work, for I had not remembered how startling good she is. Her books are not easily come by in New Zealand, but there is a copy of *Urania* in the Christchurch Public Library. This I have been re-reading with delight and wonder, finding myself moved as by no other contemporary poet. How deeply rewarding she is! At whatever level one may receive these works one does so with a profound satisfaction brought about by an absolute alliance of thought and word: here is the only way this poet could have said these things, one thinks, and it is supremely the right way.

Over and over again I have found myself arrested not only by such references as one may find to intervening poets (Blake in particular) but by a clear and strong affinity with Shakespeare's lyrics and pastoral poems. There is an unmistakeable tone made up of perception, awareness, penetration, anguish and delight, a springing ease of communication and great poetic courage: these elements seem to me to span four centuries and sound again and with authority, the Elizabethan cadence.

Others will speak knowledgeably of her position in English letters, her techniques, her sheer ability and her importance:

I speak from gratitude. When I had read the last poem in this small book, I let it fall into my lap with a sense of astonishment and very deep pleasure. Here is a great poet, I thought. It is an honour to salute her.

ECHO AND ECLOGUE

Derek Parker

Nietzsche wisely defined a joke as 'an epitaph on an emotion', and the humour in Ruth Pitter's poetry is of this order. It records, as she herself once put it, 'the smile on the face of the tiger.' As when, in A Mad Lady's Garland (1934) she recorded the song of the virtuous female spider: having devoured her husband:

> I look not here for my reward,
> But recompense shall come
> When from this toilsome life and hard
> I seek a heavenly home;
> Where in the mansions of the blest,
> By earthly ills unmarred,
> I'll meet again my Love, my best
> And sole desired reward.

The echoes are unmistakeable. And so is the tone, which pervades the book. The pious lady trout, for instance, remarks:

> How am I fed? most fitly on the fair
> Stream's self, but I myself a task have set
> To leap and snatch those sinners of the air
> That off this element presume to get;

So piously I purge the gentle sky
Of nasty atomies that dare to fly.

A few years later, in the bucolic *The Rude Potato* (1941) Miss
Pitter raised her voice a little, producing a book perhaps less
elegant, but certainly not less amusing: a relief, perhaps,
from the intensity of the two more serious intervening collections. Among these gardening poems are some of the most
amusing of her light verses; sometimes she adopts a character-
isation as far from herself as one could conceive – that, for
instance, of a Mother Weed impatiently lecturing the slow
slugs:

'You boys can get about' says she;
'Good Lor! if I could do the same,
I wouldn't leave a single tree,
Or any veg. what's worth the name;
I'm sick of all the lot of you,
The bits of damage what you do!

'Go on! 'ave them carnations down!
Climb up them roses and them beans!
Spit on them lilies, turn 'em brown,
And show what reverlootion means!' . . .

The heroic celebration of *Ruth Pitter on Cats* (1947), a decade
after Mr Eliot's practicalities, does not altogether avoid the
sentimentalities shared by most animal-lovers. But she can (as
one might have inferred from her more serious work) turn a
two-edged sword neatly upon the unwary reader, as when, in
'The Safety-Valve', she writes of a family which is determined
to give its child only reasoned affection, and so turns all the
baby talk upon the cat.

And her technical skill by this time is enormous: her
pastiche of Blake, 'Musa Translated', is entirely delightful.
Musa is a town cat, who has been transported, pregnant
and bitterly protesting, from wartime London to the country,

and popped out on the lawn to recover her tone and temper:

Trembling she croucht; but her electric Whiskers
Knew on the instant the touch of endearing Substance.
Her Eyes narrow'd; her Nostril snuft a verdurous
   Aroma;
She turn'd her Jowl sideways, and with her smooth
   cheek caress'd it,
Coarse, cutting Coxfoot-grass, the Panacea,
The Salad which is Tonick and Emetick,
And to domesticated Felines sweet and salutary.
She with immense Labour, being without true Molars,
During an Hour's Space fretted and ravell'd it,
Until the most Part of the indurated Vegetable
Had been devour'd into her urban but competent
   Stomach.
The Ball of handwrought Fibres revolving in her
   Inwards
Shortly produc'd an Upheaval: with mighty Labour
(But not forgetting to shunt in reverse to escape the
   Pollution)
She return'd it to Light, and with it slough'd her
   Sorrows,
Voided her Venom, her Hatred of man's Harlotry,
And sate for a Space compos'd, and washing her
   Whiskers.

. . .

She dream'd of prowling through the rustling Coppice,
Of slinking between the Hedgerow and the Stubble
In dry, large-moon'd Octobers; of May-mornings
When the lush moving-grass should skreen her Hunt-
   ing
And with soft Dew drench her white-velvet Bosom;
Of fishing-Expeditions in the Summer

And cosy Firesides and good Beds in Winter.
Her children should be hunters of the Mole, the stack-
Rat
And of all Vermin; her Apotheosis
Was come upon her; she had been translated.

In Miss Pitter's later work the humour has so fused with
the intensity of the speculative poems (for she is, I think,
above all a speculative poet) that each informs the other, as
when she writes (in *Still by Choice*, 1966) of Mrs Crow, who
'knew that richer people ought/To help God's good deserving
cases/And so she told them to their faces' – thereby helping
her neighbours to be charitably good. Or in the two 'Old
Nelly' poems, one half-comic, the other deeply poignant.

Humorous poems, these days, are generally sharp and
wounding: one is far more likely to come across an Adrian
Mitchell than a Ruth Pitter. Of her near-contemporaries,
perhaps only W. H. Auden (for John Betjeman is, of course,
in quite another case) cares to turn his technique to this
account. It would be unwise to say that Miss Pitter's humour
is as steadfast as her concern (in the Quaker sense) for 'the
silent music, the dance is stillness, the ineffable hints and
echoes and messages of which everything is full.' But it will
be surprising if she is not remembered at least in part for
such poems as 'The Kitten's Eclogue', which (as Hilaire Belloc
put it) display her two peculiar gifts, 'a perfect ear and exact
epithet':

My sable hue, like Ethiopian queen,
My raven tincture and my jetty dye,
Nor as defect or blemish can be seen
By anybody who hath half an eye.
What sight more welcome than the night above?
What hue more honoured in the courts of love? . . .

. . . Hold me not foul for that I wanton be;
These amorous frolics are but innocence;

101

I court no tickle immortality,
And fear no judgment when I go from hence;
No hope, no dread my little grave contains,
Nor anything beside my scant remains!

A HOMECOMING

Kathleen Raine

According to the aesthetics of Plotinus, the beautiful is a norm to which we give our immediate assent; its effect is not striking but supremely natural. The ugly and the perverse obtain notice for themselves by violation of the norm. But what they gain in immediate impact, they lose by the very fact of their lacking any correspondence with our intuitive sense of fitness; to which we return, as from sickness to health. There is in the poetry of Ruth Pitter that quality of a lost norm which strikes me, as I read her now, with the sense of homecoming to lost paradise. When I first read poems of hers, myself in my early twenties and Miss Pitter a decade older, the beautiful quiet truth of her vision seemed, to the votary of the Zeitgeist I then was, too normal to detain me. Her verse-forms, so unobtrusively skilful, were those of the main-stream of the English poetic tradition; whereas, under the impact of Eliot, Pound and the Imagists, and Herbert Read, I and my friends looked only for the novel. We were more concerned with the virtuosities of Joyce, wresting new mean-ings from words by taking the language apart, than with pre-serving, as Miss Pitter does, the English words in their full-ness of connotation. Her 'nature' poetry, stemming from the

Georgian poets against whom my generation was in reaction, described a poetic landscape so familiar that we had forgotten that it was the poets, from Spenser and Milton and Herrick, to de la Mare, Hardy, and Hopkins, who had created it and kept it green. Honour and poverty (the two virtues Ruth Pitter praises) seemed in the thirties less interesting than the various postures of the *non serviam* at that time offered us – the 'pure psychic automatism' of Surrealism; the anti-beauty of leftist social realism; the skeletal laconism of Imagist free-verse; Empsonian cerebral complexity; Sitwellian exoticism. Her very Englishness then semed a fault, for internationalism was a political vogue. There have been other avant-gardisms since – the respective 'truthfulnesses' of the obscene, the plebeian, the ironic, and the bottomless self-pity of a neurotic subjectivism.

Mercifully time sets us right; every avant-garde becomes an old guard in the course of nature. Miss Pitter, never in any fashion, is no more out-of-date now than those other accomplished poets by whose perfect use of the English language she has 'trued' her style; as she has 'trued' her eye by the perennial earth and its creatures, and her inward vision by the perennial nature of the human soul. Her sense of joy, her acceptance of sorrow (attitudes alike shocking to the revolutionary morality) seem, as I read her now, the fruits of a knowledge far deeper than those showy postures of cynicism and despair whose only ground is ignorance.

Poem after poem I have come upon in her collected volume which I have wished I had written myself: 'Dear Perfection' (with the perfection of Herbert); 'The Viper'; 'Stormcock in Elder'; 'If you Came'; 'The Bird in the Tree'; 'Hoverfly on Poppy'; 'The Bat'; 'But For Lust'; 'Dew'; 'The Lammastide Flower'; and 'Morning Glory'. Again and again her eye sees so exactly snapdragon and harebell, viper and spider and jackdaw, yew-tree and leaf-cutting bee, that envy is disarmed by pleasure in her excellence.

She can be exotic on occasion:

For there abides the torrent of golden wire,
The silver silk, the cactus-anther river,
The rose-death purple mantled on with fire.

Her dream poems too are 'trued' to a reality we recognise, while marvelling at the rightness of the words in which she evokes the landscape of that other world of consciousness. She explores a whole range of solitudes Emily Bronte would have recognised.

Ruth Pitter is a born poet; the medium of verse is, one feels, her native element. If I write rather of her content than of her technique, it is because she herself understands that a poem

'begins and ends in mystery. It begins in that secret movement of the poet's being, in response to the secret dynamism of life.'

Another fashion of my generation was to define a poem as 'the words on the page', as if a heap of words could somehow generate meaning. Every poet worth the name knows that the poem is a whole before the parts are drawn into its magnetic field; a living essence to which the words are 'true'. Those who doubt her technical inventiveness have only to read her light verse, which reveals an almost too great abundance of verbal inventiveness, held, in her best work, under strict control.

Nor has the avant-garde any more insight into contemporary events than has the quiet observer. Among war poems of the last war, 'The Cygnet' deserves to stand with Edwin Muir's 'The Good Town' and Dylan Thomas's 'Ceremony After a Fire Raid'. She is aware too of the industrial landscape and of the common people; whom she sees, however, not as some new species or unprecedented phenomenon, but, as in 'Flowers in the Factory', 'Funeral Wreaths', or 'Old, Childless, Husbandless', as a Christian sees fellow-souls in a world hard at all times; these too she 'trues' to the human norm.

Her range is far greater than those suppose, who think of her as a minor Georgian poet: long reflective poems, like 'May 1947', 'Exercise in the Pathetic Fallacy', 'Thanksgiving for a Fair Summer', place her with the Metaphysical poets not in style only (which can be imitated) but in their kind and quality of vision, which cannot. Having reread her, I now see her as one of the poets whose best work will survive as long as the English language, with whose expressiveness in image and idea she has kept faith, remains.

AUTHORITY AND ELEGANCE

Robin Skelton

Ruth Pitter had been silent for a long while before the welcome appearance in 1966 of her volume *Still by Choice*. She is not a fashionable poet; her verses are often neatly turned and metrically smooth; her syntax is largely conventional and her epithets are unsurprising. Nevertheless, she contrives to delight and startle with the precision of her structures and the real elegance of her perception.

It may seem odd to suggest that Miss Pitter, who was born in 1897, is part of the changing direction of British poetry, but it is as true of her as it is of Robert Graves who is two years older. Like him she indulges, from time to time, in the mannerism of a deft inversion. Like him she balances lucid colloquialism against an occasional archaism. Her imagery, like his, makes use of the pastoral English tradition as well as of the classical. And her poems, like his, succeed because of the authority and elegance of their structures, as much as because of their sensibility and profundity.

A number of fragments from *Still by Choice* may indicate what I mean. There is the vivid, beautifully controlled opening of 'Moths and Mercury-vapour Lamp':

> Some beat the glass as if in agony,
> The pattern never still enough to see;

In the unearthly strong cold radiance
Eyes glitter, wings are flourished, weapons glance,
Furs, metals, dyes; duellers with flashing foils
Glitter like fire and struggle in the toils
Of potent light, as deep-sea fish are drawn
From profound dark to anguish and the dawn.

In this the restrained, almost obvious epithets give the poem a degree of distance and enable the tone to remain assured, and the concluding generalisation to achieve a climax without melodrama. The closing lines of the poem illustrate the metaphysical passion of Miss Pitter's vision:

With eyes of night or diamond turned my way
Upright, as crucified upon the glass,
That strong invisible they cannot pass,
For ever watching at the terrible gate
Until the writing shall be read, they wait.

The phrase 'that strong invisible' may remind us of George Herbert; and if Graves occasionally recalls Carew and the Cavaliers, Miss Pitter recalls Herbert, Vaughan, and the metaphysicals. Sometimes there is an elegant chill foreboding, as in the last stanza of 'Morning Glory' – a beautifully ironic title:

And there is one thing more; as in despair
The eye dwells on that ribbed octagonal round,
A cold sidereal whisper brushes the ear,
A prescient tingling, a prophecy of sound.

Miss Pitter is not always thus poised. In 'Who Knows' she handles colloquialism within rhyming couplets with a deftness amounting to effrontery. In 'The Irish Patriarch' she displays both whimsy and gusto. In 'Night Flower Piece', an analysis of a romantic painting, she achieves a wholly individual and idiosyncratic tone. The last three stanzas of this poem seem to me to reveal true mastery of technique and real profundity of vision:

What more can I discover
Now reconciled to purely tragic reading?
There is the dying lover,
Dark-clotted, leaning over;
Amaranth – the common name is love-lies-bleeding.

The spider and the snail
Nocturnal, self-enclosed and self-secreting,
Close web and slimy trail,
Work coldly in the pale
Ghost-glimmer, co-existing but not meeting.

What is behind that wall,
A palace, or a fortress, or a town?
Over the rampart tall,
From shade funereal,
The hawk-faced heathen sentinel looks down.

Ruth Pitter is clearly a major poet, and speaking to our time and all times.

SUDDENLY I SAW

Robert Speaight

It is more than thirty years since James Stephens and Hilaire Belloc commended Ruth Pitter to English readers. Belloc praised her 'perfect ear' and her command of the 'exact epithet'. In A *Trophy of Arms* you will find winter evoked by the 'dry bents' hissing in the 'raving air'; the 'smutted ear' lying in the furrow; the 'swagging heap of swollen cloud'. Yeats had written of 'raving autumn'; and Stephens did not hesitate to put Ruth Pitter with Yeats, if an inch or two below him. Here is language as Hopkins used it: the same anchorage in the concrete; the same leap from matter which can be described exactly, to spirit which cannot be described at all. For if her sensitive and accurate observation of nature aligns Miss Pitter with poets like Clare and Edward Thomas, her intuition of a divine purpose places her in the company of Henry Vaughan:

> The starling perched upon the tree
> With his long tress of straw –
> When suddenly heaven blazed on me,
> And suddenly I saw . . .

or the angel that shines 'apparelled in eternity'. Here is a genuine mystical vision, effortlessly translated into verse. It is comforting to meet a poet who has turned her back upon 'the reasoned pathways to despair'; and the pathways are no longer so reasoned as they were when she learnt to shun them.

Remote from fashion, and undeservedly remote from fame, the lasting quality of Miss Pitter's verse is guaranteed by her precise use both of images and ideas. She can be exalted, as she can also be amusing; but she is never vague.

THE HIDDEN HEART

Hallam Tennyson

The Rude Potato by Ruth Pitter: the time was 1941, I was
twenty, Europe was enflamed. The name of the author seemed
as raw, tuberous, uncompromising as her title. At such a
moment it was reassuring to find an earth-mother of this
tough, vegetable fibre, a muse in jodhpurs wielding not a pen
but a pruning hook. Looking at the poems today in isolation
from Ruth Pitter's other work, it is hard to remember the
reasons why they should have helped to rekindle a faith in
life which had grown despondent and sickly: for now they
seem no more than a series of first-rate *Punch* jokes. Yet at
the time they *were* a tremendous affirmation, made not from
any ivory tower but from a deep involvement with life at its
most common or garden. Miss Pitter has always seen the 'spirit
of comedy' as one of the Great Trinity: 'smaller than they
but not less mysterious . . . refusing to be exterminated or left
behind.'

Until we met in 1957 *The Rude Potato* was all I knew of
her work. Then, when we did meet, the image the book had
imposed on my mind was, so I discovered, wildly inaccurate.
She wore no jodhpurs but a neat two-piece, a string of pearls,
a careful hat: and instead of a pint- swilling farmer's daughter
I was confronted by someone shy but fearless, sharp (she dis-
missed one well-known poet because his ears were too small)

112

yet deeply compassionate. Since that first meeting Miss Pitter's poetry has never ceased to fascinate and its wholeness, its integrity, its exact expression of a complete personal attitude to life, has gradually impressed itself as likely to take its place as one of the few lasting contributions to poetry made since 1930.

Ruth Pitter deprecates any false discrimination between the sexes, and yet the woman poet does occupy a peculiarly exposed position. Men are past masters at having their cake and eating it: they can abandon themselves to their sensual and emotional natures and yet keep a sanctuary for tranquil recollection. Biologically this separatism is much more difficult for women and for them the cost of dedication to the muse has often had a crippling effect. One thinks of Emily Dickinson, immured in her white room, Christina Rossetti cultivating an ingrowing virginity, Emily Bronte's early death, and others nearer our time, each afflicted with her own vanity or odd-ness. But Miss Pitter is not odd, nor ingrown, nor vain, nor even dead. She is full of common sense, and at seventy-one years young is involved with the life around her in half a dozen practical and ordinary ways. This achievement is of tremendous importance to our understanding of her poetry and indeed it is central to the very nature of her poetic output. Her poetry is an expression of balance – not the calm external appearance of balance which we find in a Pindaric Ode nor the imposed, literary, artificial balance of the Georgians. It is a balance which comes not from denying or suppressing inner tensions, but from transcending them. And its achievement is no less costly though it may be less spectacular than the more personal distresses to which other women poets have succumbed.

Miss Pitter is quite frank about the cost. Her last volume of new poems contained one of her most beautiful and heart-rending lyrics 'The Heart's Desire is Full of Sleep':

> The heart's desire is full of sleep,
> For men who have their will

Have gained a good they cannot keep,
And must go down the hill

Not questioning the seas and skies,
Not questioning the years;
For life itself has closed their eyes,
And life has stopped their ears.

But some, true emperors of desire,
True heirs to all regret,
Strangers and pilgrims, still enquire
For what they never get;

For what they know is not on earth
They seek until they find;
The children hopeful in their mirth,
The old but part resigned.

And though they cannot see love's face
They tread his former track;
They know him by his empty place,
They know him by their lack.

I seek the company of such,
I wear that worn attire;
For I am one who has had much,
But not the heart's desire.

To see so clearly the price she has paid for rejecting the
heart's desire and to enumerate with such precision the
emotional comforts which she has forfeited is an extraordinary
achievement. Of course there is regret, without it such a poem
could scarcely have been written: but the triumph trans-
cends this regret. She is not 'full of sleep' but must press on
to new discoveries, new truths. The poem's balance comes

from this perfect fusion of triumph and regret and the way in which the tension and conflict are sublimated in the very moment that they achieve expression.

Think not that I complain that I must go
Under the ground, unblossomed, unfulfilled

she writes in an earlier poem. Indeed no, 'complain' is something that Miss Pitter never does. Her objectivity, her sublimation of direct personal emotion in her poetry, are thus not the result of a coldness or of a lack of heart. This one poem would be enough to show us that. Poetry itself has been a mystical discipline for her, and as with all the most creative mystics this discipline has led her *towards* an ever deeper understanding of the natural world and not *away* from it. This is where the rude potato comes in. Wherever Ruth Pitter has been able to participate in everyday life without violating her core of reserve and creativity she *has* participated and with gusto. Her response to animals, to plants, to nature has always been of the most unsentimental and yet joyful kind. Where Emily Dickinson felt 'Zero at the bone' on seeing a viper, Ruth Pitter feels an immediate wonder at 'the fallen angel's comeliness'. She is delighted to find a bat 'warm as milk' with 'thin translucent ears'; and a vine in bloom soothes her with its promise of a continuity that goes beyond the span of human life. This theme of the eternal continuity of nature, stretching back to the past as well as forward into the future, is recurring: there is a wonderfully exact childhood recollection, 'Herding Lambs', in which the figures, although the image is scarcely more than touched on, seem to have merged with the decorations on an Attic vase.

Man, then, is part of this enduring process, a process larger than he himself, a process that is at times frightening, at times terrible, at times funny – but if seen clearly and truthfully, a process that is always beautiful. Even in moments of agony the truth reasserts itself.

And yet the secret stream of grace
Flows on, and swells the same,
As if from out another place
Where sorrow has no name.

And in her long and magnificent poem 'The Cygnet', which
was prompted by her work in a London factory during the
blitz, she celebrates this indestructible forward movement of
life in a world temporarily clogged by misery and madness.
Again, who but Ruth Pitter could have seen that under his
waxed moustache and his dreams of 'interracial fornications'
the Military Harpist was soul-mate to the 'beloved poet of
Israel?' Even the savage irony of 'Funeral Wreaths' ends on a
note of hope and compassion:

> The gibbetted carnations with steel wires thrust
> Right through their rankling midriffs, the skewered
>   roses,
> Tulips turned inside-out for a bolder show,
> Arum lilies stuck upright in tortured poses
> Like little lavatory-basins – these victims grow
> In a private garden for each, in a heavenly soil.
> Mindless and pagan offering, wicked waste,
> This is the efflorescence of godless toil,
> Something that has no meaning, that has no taste,
> Something that has no use but to cry aloud,
> Going up to the gates of life with a formless din,
> 'We are the lost, betrayed ones. We are the Crowd.
> Think, for you must do something to let us in.'

I do not want to leave the impression that Miss Pitter's
poetry moves me primarily because of the view of life, the
moral content, that it expresses; for this element in her poetry
is not significant in itself. Its significance comes as I have tried
to point out from the absolute honesty with which it is expressed. And this honesty of attitude is matched by an equal
honesty of language. Miss Pitter's images are never dragged in

for effect. At first there was a certain tendency to the romantic
and the archaic – 'eldritch,' 'sere' and inversions ('She reared
not up the heath among') that remind one of 'The Lady of
Shalott': but these have disappeared. The diction has become
more chaste, the words more precise and apt: there is little
contemporary demotic speech,* however, and no metaphors
drawn from cars, atoms, skyscrapers, or even electricity. The
vocabulary remains firmly diatonic with hardly a word that
Wordsworth or Blake could not have used. This language,
which is, of course, manipulated with great subtlety and
grace, may, in the long run, come to seem much more timeless and eternal than the series of ephemeral shocks initiated
by Eliot's 'Patient etherised upon a table.'

Miss Pitter's unfaltering sense of rhythm is perhaps even
more remarkable than her use of language. 'The Military
Harpist' and 'The Cygnet' employ unrhymed metres of vary-
ing lengths whose internal rhythms and alternating weak
and strong endings follow an instinctive pattern which is
hard to analyse but entirely satisfying. Elsewhere there are
many kinds of rhyme sequence, and an extraordinary variety
of metres which remind one here of Greek and there of biblical
originals. Miss Pitter was taught to recite by her schoolteacher
parents from the age of six and seems to have a knowledge
of the exact quantity of every word (could she have told

* Editor: 'Little contemporary demotic speech?' True enough in a
sense; but one does not need to turn to her comic verse for examples
of a masterly use of the colloquial. Others in this book have noted
how she uses it sometimes for contrast. Sometimes too she uses it,
slightly heightened or distilled, for a whole serious poem: 'Yorkshire
Wife's Saga' is one example. In 'The Stolen Babe', with a deceptive
air of simplicity and without rhyme or formal structure, she shapes
plain speech into a poignant music:

> Ah, I know she's ailing, that's what kills me.
> She's not like us, and I don't know what to do.
> I'd take her to a hospital, but I don't trust 'em.
> Besides, she's so white, they'd know I'd stole her.
> Ah sleep, my lovey! sleep, my lily!
> Tired to death she is, but she ain't crying;
> She's one of them that's too proud to complain.

Tennyson how to scan 'scissors,' the one word in English over which he admitted defeat?). Her organisation of language beautifully matches the organisation of life and heart which has made her poetry possible. Most wonderful of all, perhaps, when a poem demands absolute simplicity of treatment she frees herself from this elaborate diction and achieves miracles of economy and discipline that reach unerringly into the heart:

> If you came to my secret glade,
> 	Weary with heat,
> I would set you down in the shade,
> 	I would wash your feet.

> If you came in the winter sad,
> 	Wanting for bread,
> I would give you the last that I had,
> 	I would give you my bed.

> But the place is hidden apart
> 	Like a nest by a brook,
> And I will not show you my heart
> 	By a word, by a look.

> The place is hidden apart
> 	Like the nest of a bird:
> And I will not show you my heart
> 	By a look, by a word.

Reading this poem in an earlier volume (it was first published in 1939) one might have been forgiven for thinking it a brilliant pastiche of Christina Rossetti: another virgin poetess lamenting her solitude. It is Miss Pitter's triumph to have proved such a judgment totally wrong. The heart that was being hidden was to be kept for deeper, fuller and less

limited experiences than Christina knew: and because of
that it is still unsleeping, still alert:

> To say, or even to see,
>   For a moment of time,
> What the Tree and the Bird must be
>   In the true sublime.

POET OF LIVING FORM

John Wain

Ruth Pitter at seventy-one has the brisk step and good com-
plexion of a healthy woman of fifty. She spends many hours
each day out of doors, tending her plants; and she has always
worked a good deal with her hands. These facts will surprise
no one. They could be deduced by any attentive reader of her
poetry. Not only because of what we see at first glance – that
this is a poetry that concerns itself with 'nature' – but because of what we see on second and subsequent glances, that
this is the poetry of someone accustomed to working at a
craft. Ruth Pitter does not merely string words together, or
throw them up in heaps: she shapes them.

   At the present moment, this quality is out of fashion. How
could it be anything else, in the world we inhabit now? From
California to Chelsea, from Oslo to Tokyo, the young writers
and readers of poetry are reared in a world where everything
they see, handle or use is made in a factory, and generally
made out of plastics. Their sensibility is attuned to the flow
of traffic along a road, the flow of manufactured things from
an assembly line. Consequently, they enjoy language that
goes on in an endless stream until it ceases at the flick of a
switch. Nothing is meant to be lingered over; no rhythm, no

word, is chosen because it is felicitous; the only quality demanded is this endless flow.

It all takes us back to those lines of Ezra Pound's:

All things are a flowing
Sage Heraclitus says:
But a tawdry cheapness
Shall outlast our days.

We have them both all round us, the flowing and the tawdry cheapness. Personally, I believe that there will be a reaction, a swing of the pendulum. This flow-writing is so diabolically boring that people cannot stand it for long. Up to now, their answer, when they find that they cannot stand it, is to give up reading altogether, to abandon literacy, to let language slide in the way that television lets it slide. If the entire human race goes on doing this, language will rot and thought will rot with it. But I do not believe they will go on. I believe that language consciously used, shaped like a living material into living form, will reassert its hold on the human mind. After all, we have seen periods like this before. In the middle stretch of the sixteenth century, as in the middle stretch of the twentieth, the arts that depended on language sank to a very low ebb. Greatness flowed into painting, into architecture, into music; but there was little of any interest in literature. Who, in 1550, would have believed you if you had predicted Shakespeare, Marlowe and Donne, all writing before the century ended?

The warmth of the tributes to Ruth Pitter, the excitement generated by her big new collection, seems to me to illustrate this. She is a poet of living form. Everywhere in her work, one sees the marks of a sensibility formed by the struggle with real materials: with wood, with paint, with soil and water and tendrils and leaves. This kind of work cannot be produced by someone whose life has been lived among abstractions, who knows only those realities that can be theorised into being. When Ruth Pitter goes to her desk to write a poem, she is motivated by love – not only by love of created life, but by love of language, of rhyme, of the matching of texture and weight and pace against what is to be said. She does not make, and does not allow her readers to make, the mistake of imagining that it is possible to love the soul of poetry without also loving its body.

Ruth Pitter is a poet of the full singing voice. She has other veins too; some of her work is casual, relaxed, sly in its ironies. But I like her best when she is putting on singing-robes. She writes the high style naturally, and there is no need for her to come down to familiarity in order to convince us that what she is saying concerns our lives. C. S. Lewis, in his book on sixteenth-century English literature, makes a distinction between the 'drab' and the 'golden' in poetry. By 'drab' he means to indicate a diction and a rhythm that deliberately put on humble clothing, that avoid direct rhetorical or lyrical flights, that prefer the interrupted rhythm, the oblique verbal effect, the low key. By 'golden', Lewis means the opposite of these: the poetry that soars, sings, wears scarlet and gold, delights in a straightforward confrontation of experience, goes delightedly head-on into the experience it deals with. (Lewis claimed that these terms are neutrally descriptive and did not imply any judgment of value on his part, but since he so obviously prefered Golden to Drab it is hard to accept this altogether.) I mention the matter because I recently heard a broadcast lecture by W. H. Auden in which he took these terms over from Lewis and applied them to modern poetry. He himself, said Auden, was a 'drab' poet, and what was more, every modern poet he admired was 'drab' also. He confessed that no modern poet who spoke with a raised voice inspired him with anything but embarrassment.

I honour Auden for stating his point of view so clearly and being too big a man to hide behind equivocations. But his judgment seems to me an unfortunate one. Rob modern poetry of its 'golden' note, of its poets who raise their voices and speak above a mumble, and you throw away some of the best

of Yeats, virtually all of Dylan Thomas, the love poems of
Theodore Roethke, the most urgent and compelling of Robert
Lowell's poems, and indeed some short but memorable flights
in the poetry of Mr Auden himself. You also throw away the
finest work of Ruth Pitter; and this, we are in no mood to
permit.

> Give me the bird of Paradise, though dying,
> Exiled and doomed, ravished from the Elysian
> Forest where I shall never see it flying,
> Where Cœlogyne flowers like a vision:
> Never shall hear the love-tormented crying.
>
> For there abides the torrent of golden wire,
> The silver silk, the cactus-anther river,
> The rose-death purple mantled on with fire,
> The dying-dolphin green where lightnings quiver,
> The trembling arches of the silent lyre.
>
> Though I shall never see the sudden turning
> Into a sphery monstrance, globe of splendour,
> The ecstasy that is beyond our learning,
> The action and the attitude that render
> Love back to whence it came, the phoenix burning:
>
> Though I shall never hear, rending assunder
> The bonds that trammel love, that cry of passion,
> The voice that is more terrible than thunder:
> Though at its death my life be desolation,
> Give me the bird of paradise, the wonder.

There is another successful vein in Ruth Pitter's work: a
vein of high extravagance. It is not quite (in Lewis's sense)
'golden'. It is lofty but at the same time streaked with irony:
or, if not exactly irony, then with something intellectual and
self-mocking, something powerfully at work to assimilate the

doubts and hesitations it cannot help encountering, even generating. It is this side of her work that aligns her with Donne. We find it, for instance, in 'The Military Harpist'. This is a poem almost sardonic, its portrait almost a grotesque : yet no other method would suffice to say the rich and complex things the poem is saying :

> He is now where his bunion has no existence.
> Breathing an atmosphere free of pipeclay and swearing,
> He wears the starched nightshirt of the hereafter, his
> halo
> Is plain manly brass with a permanent polish,
> Requiring no oily rag and no Soldier's Friend.

> His place is with the beloved poet of Israel,
> With the wandering minnesinger and the loves of
> Provence,
> With Blondel footsore and heartsore, the voice in the
> darkness
> Crying like beauty bereaved beneath many a donjon,
> O Richard ! O king ! where is the lion of England?
> With Howell, Llewellyn, and far in the feral north
> With the savage fame of the hero in glen and in ben,
> At the morning discourse of saints in the island Eire,
> And at nameless doings in the stone-circle, the dreadful
> grove.

A poem like that makes real to me one of the most difficult passages in Ruth Pitter's latest statement about her own work, the Preface to her new collection. 'I have had', she says, 'strange thoughts at times about comedy. Imagine a comic work, or try to imagine the possibility of a comic work, as majestic as our loftiest tragedies; a laughter as august as the almost unbearable nobility of *Oedipus*.' In the abstract, I find it impossible to imagine any such thing. But a poem like 'The Military Harpist' brings humour into the very centre of a grave, compassionate, yet delighted, view of the human condition.

Thus far into the dark do I delve for his likeness:
He harps at the Druid sacrifice, where the golden string
Sings to the golden knife and the victim's shriek.
Strangely assorted, the shape of song and the bloody
    man.

There, cruelty and terror and laughter and joy all come
together.

THE GREAT TRADITION

John Hall Wheelock

I was delighted to learn of the publication of *Poems 1926–1966* by Ruth Pitter, surely one of the truest, the most accomplished, and the most poignant lyric poets of our era. Long before I had the honour of meeting her, I had fallen under the spell of her poetry, and knew many of her poems by heart. I still know many of them by heart – the best of them are unforgettable. If I should have the great pleasure of seeing her again, I don't doubt I should again run the risk of boring her – as I once did in a railway carriage in transit from somewhere to London – by reciting her own poetry to her. Has any poet of our time written anything more perfect, or more perfectly sustained, than 'The Cygnet' or more profound than 'Passion and Peace'?

> Poetry, like all passion, seeks for peace.
> Wild creature, look into the pool and learn.
> There in the level water shines the face,
> The summer eyes that can both weep and burn,
> Mirrored so calmly in the quiet place;
> Fire in sweet water lulled, questions that turn
> At long last to the simple need for rest.
> Have I not still the peace of the unborn,
> Have I not learnt of death to be possessed?

O put off passion, and with passion scorn,
And think that this quiet water is my breast,
Calm, yet without that image, most forlorn.
O let the fervour of the princely sun,
Which makes the desert solitary, sleep
Here in the water his dominions weep,
Binding all peace and passion into one.

There, by means of a superb metaphor, a miracle is achieved: the synthesis of two opposites, opening immeasurable vistas to the imagination.

In Ruth Pitter, the great tradition has found a creative interpreter, an original voice.

Tailpiece on Behalf of Humbler Creators

Poet, don't trouble to return
Our verses – let them stay, or burn
They would be proud to stay
Even in your woodshed, even half a day.
How could they find a fate prouder or fitter
Than kindling a bonfire for Ruth Pitter?   AWR.